THE DREAMER'S JOURNEY
Push Past Your Fears and Pursue Your Dreams

Thomas C. Lynch

Published By: Dream2Inspire, LLC.
Copyright © 2017 Thomas C. Lynch
All rights reserved.

ISBN: 0692847588
ISBN-13: 978-0692847589

CONTENTS

DEDICATION

First and foremost, I thank God and the higher energy force, which continues to flow in and out of everything in existence. I am so grateful and honored to be blessed with such a beautiful vision and purpose for my life. The purpose I discovered for my life came to me in the form of a dream. That dream was to inspire. That dream became my focus and has allowed me to help transform and inspire many lives around the world. I truly and full-heartedly love what I do and do what I love. I believe we all have visions for our lives. It is our mission to pursue and experience the things we desire that fulfill us. You only have this moment right here, right now. The future is not guaranteed and no other moment in the past can be relived. All you have is the present moment to pursue those things you desire in your heart.

To my mother, thank you for your love and support. You have always been my inspiration. It is because of you that I learned how to bring people together in a harmonious way with love and lasting relationships. You are one of the strongest people I know. I love you and appreciate everything you have instilled in me.

To my father, thank you for your love and support. You have also been my inspiration. I learned from you how to become a man of honor and respect others while commanding respect in return. You are also one of the strongest people I know. I love you and appreciate everything you have instilled in me.

To my brother from a different mother, my cousin Amir, a.k.a. Amircle. Throughout the years, we have helped each other along our journeys. You showed me that there was more to life than what I had been used to. We grew up together. You gave me an opportunity to grow and learn more about my journey and myself. I am truly thankful for our "cousinship."

Along every journey, there are great influencers and spiritual guides who are placed in your life to keep you on track to achieving your life purpose and goals. Thank you, Tracy and Amanda, for your continued support. Thank you, Aunt Carolyn, for your advice and guidance. You continue to inspire me. Thank you to all of my beautiful aunts, cousins, and family for your love and support. Thank you to my friends Gill, Stephon, Larry, Montae, Erik, Keaver B., Brian S., David R., and Peter G. —as well as my mentors and coaches Johnny Campbell a.k.a. "The Transition Man", Andrew Chiu, Mel Austin, and Djoser G-Q. All of you have played a key role along my journey. I truly appreciate your support and guidance along my journey.

Inspirational Moment with TL

Fear to pursue your dreams is like covering your eyes and being afraid of darkness, but not realizing you're the one creating the darkness.

INTRODUCTION

Have you ever felt like you are spending countless years of irreversible time working a job you hate? Have you ever wanted to quit your job but were too afraid of the consequences? Do you have a burning desire to experience a different lifestyle? What are you passionate about? What skills and talents do you already have that you haven't used to your advantage so that you can experience the lifestyle you want? How many days are you going to continue the same mundane routines before you take action?

These are the thoughts I struggled with over a thousand times in my head for fifteen years of my life. I had been living my life acting as a mechanical robot. I felt I was living without purpose, just existing in the world around me doing things I was told to do because that was "the way it is." For most of my life, I never really questioned it either. Like most people, I was following the blueprint society says we must follow. We are taught that we are to graduate high school and go to college to become doctors or lawyers or working professionals—to major in any subject so we can later get a job working for someone else. We are expected to get a bachelor's or master's degree to have a competitive edge with the most potential of getting a high-paying, "secure" job. Then once we graduate and find a job, we are expected to spend thirty-plus years working until we either retire or die. We feel the pressures of family and society to achieve these things from an early age. From childhood to adulthood, we are pressured by the beliefs and expectations of our families, peers, and society to follow the status quo. It is because we try to meet others' expectations that we lose a sense of what matters to us. Following the expectations of others our whole lives, we eventually struggle to identify who we are.

Many of us are conditioned from the early stages of life to think a certain way, talk a certain way, look a certain way, act a certain way, or behave a certain way. The more we follow the status quo and try to keep up with what everyone else is doing, the bigger our egos grow. We compare and often cast judgment on others and ourselves. Eventually, our self-awareness fades, and we forget what matters. It's as if we are sleepwalking through life with no sense of purpose. We are constantly competing with what society views as acceptable and trying to fit within the limits of what is considered "normal." However, what your parents say, what society says, and what other people think is not the truth about your life. If you discover your truth, you will wake up. It's like waking a sleeping giant. Once you wake up from all the noise around you, you will discover who you truly are meant to be. If you continue to stay asleep, you will always be dreaming of who you could become.

No one decides how you live your life. Most parents try to put their children on the right path based on what they believe is good for their children. Their beliefs are influenced by their past experiences, failures, and fears. In some cases, this is a great thing. It will keep their children from damaging their lives and futures. On the other hand, their fears could be dream killers for their children, and their children may have a hard time identifying who they are because they are living in their parents' vision of what their lives should be. Ultimately your life is *your* life. You are the only one who will face great pain and discontent by living someone else's vision for your life.

Then one day, you will wake up in your elderly years, looking back on all the things you could have done, all the chances you could have taken, and all the opportunities you allowed to pass by. Then suddenly, you fall to your knees, crying in anguish and disappointment because you are coming to terms with the fact that you are now approaching the end of your life. You realize you will never get to know who you are or the full potential to create the life you've always dreamed of. Just as you are about to take your last breath, you finally admit you allowed fear and lack of taking action on your dream to decide your fate. When you get to this point, it is too late. You will never become the person you desire to be. You will never have the experiences you desire for your life.

Not too exciting, right? Decide right now to break free from the barriers of fear, and begin to take a risk to bet on yourself and your potential. You have something burning deep inside you that wants to explode. The life you desire can be created when you decide to take a chance and follow your heart. You can make your dreams a reality if you understand the fears you have for pursuing your dreams, identify what you need to do to tackle your fears, identify what you want to achieve, and take consistent action to push past those fears to become the person you are truly meant to be for the success of your dream.

I must warn you—pushing past your fears to pursue your dreams is not easy. This is because it is mostly a battle of the mind where the victim and the hero are the same person. I'm not trying to discourage you. I am simply stating a fact. Some moments along your journey will feel tough to handle. You will doubt yourself. There will be struggles and uncomfortable feelings of uncertainty and stress. The good news is that you have control over how you respond to your fears and challenges. It is important to understand that being afraid of something new is a part of the process. You can learn how to control your fears by identifying them and taking action. The decision to take action despite fear pushes you forward to achieving your dreams. The lessons you learn as a result of facing your fears about life, your boundaries, your character, your vision, your mindset, and your potential will help you push forward to succeed along your journey.

Two common reasons why most people fail to accomplish major goals are fear and self-doubt. We fail our goals by never taking risks for ourselves and by allowing fear to control us. We fail ourselves when we let our insecurities rule our decisions and impede our actions. If you are unaware of this in yourself, it could lead you to believe you are a victim. The reality of it is you have complete control over how you think and how you respond to your fears. To push past your fears to pursue your dreams, you have to trust in your ability to overcome whatever comes your way.

My definition of "fear" is "false expectations affecting results." The truth is, fear is a dream killer. Some of the most common fears we allow to prevent us from pursuing a dream are the fear of failure, change, not being good enough, the unknown, judgment, rejection, and success. These fears are the reason why so many people go to their graves never seeing their dreams become a reality.

How many times have you wanted to do something but the fear of failure, change, not being good enough, the unknown, judgment, rejection, or success created a barrier for you that you found almost impossible to get over?

Fear paralyzes its victims and distorts their perception. Fear influences how you respond to situations. Fear can even affect how you view yourself and the world around you. In my opinion, it's one of the many epidemics affecting the quality of life for most people. If only we allowed ourselves to control how we respond to our fears, we would be free. We would discover a source within us that is indestructible if we maintained control of it.

This book will help you strengthen your connection with yourself and your dreams. You will learn how to identify your dreams, goals, and passions, as well as your fears about pursuing these things. You will be able to effectively respond to your dreams and your fears after completing this book. It is time for you to push past your fears to pursue your Dreamer's Journey. Along this journey, I will share with you my story of what led me to finally face my fears to pursue my dreams. You will also learn about the "Seven Deadly Fears That Will Kill Your Dreams." Later, I will talk about the "Ten Ways to Push Past Your Fears", as well as other useful tools to help you push past your fears and pursue your dreams.

You will read about the series of events leading to my decision to quit my job at one of the largest entertainment companies in the world and pursue my dreams of becoming an entrepreneur, inspirational speaker, and author. I will share my experiences, challenges, and lessons along the way of pursuing my dreams, with the hopes of inspiring you to pursue your dreams. These experiences, challenges, and lessons have transformed my life and have empowered me to push past my fears to pursue my dreams.

One thing to note: this book is not about convincing you to quit your job. I am willing to bet I don't need to convince you to quit your job, but if you hate what you're doing for a living, move on to something else. Life is too short to be miserable. I believe a major part of your mission in life is to fulfill your life with the work you love to do. I would also bet on the reason why you are reading this book, is because you may be at the point of wanting more for your life. Is it possible what you are currently doing is no longer fulfilling? Maybe you want to quit your job and want to know how someone else was able to do it and still survive. Either way my hope is by sharing my experiences of discovering myself and pursuing my dreams will help you realize it's time to take action to pursue what you love. Use this book to examine your life so that you can align with what you truly desire to be, do, or have for your life.

If you decide you want to quit your job after reading this book to pursue a dream, that is your choice, and only you can make that choice unless you get fired. Regardless of what you decide, one thing is certain; you can never go wrong when you follow your heart and pursue your dreams.

Inspirational Moment with TL

A dream is what you visualize and think about all day. Passion is
something you feel that will drive you to create your dream.

CHAPTER ONE: SOMETHING ELSE OUT THERE

What is your dream? Do you want to live life on your terms by doing the work you love? Do you want to become a teacher, a lawyer, a doctor, an actor, an author, or own a business? Do you want to become financially free? Whatever dreams you have, I believe those things are meant for you. One of my dreams is to achieve financial freedom through my creativity, ideas, talent, skills, and efforts. I want to push past my fears and pursue my dreams of being a transformational inspirational speaker, coach, and successful entrepreneur. As an inspirational speaker, my dream, as well as the motivation behind writing this book, is to help push you toward your dreams, your potential, and your passion. To help you identify all self-imposed limitations preventing you from taking the first step towards pursuing your dreams. As a public speaking coach, my dream is to help millions of people around the world develop their public speaking skills. I want to help speakers discover their true authentic self-expression to build self-confidence with public speaking. I do this by showing you how to share your ideas and use your body language, voice, storytelling abilities, and message to effectively engage your audience. As an entrepreneur, my dream is to own successful businesses and create wealth for my family.

One of the smartest strategies in the world for becoming financially free is finding what you love to do and getting paid for it. I know what it's like to be completely broke with a job or without a job. Both suck. Money isn't everything but it is a necessity. The more you have the more you can experience and create with. I want to be my own boss and live life on my own terms because no one on the Forbes Top 100 is an employee. As an employee, my plan for earning more money was to either win the lottery or work a lot of overtime. I planned to work for ten to fifteen years to earn a promotion to a top-level position and retire after thirty years. I used to think this was the best strategy to earn more money. I once thought if I became a Vice

President of the company, it would result in becoming financially free. My backup plan was to win the Mega Millions. Fifteen years later I realized my plans were flawed. I still wanted to be financially free, but I felt further away from it.

In my opinion, financial freedom means you have the freedom to do what you want at any given moment because money is no longer a concern. It means no debt, all your bills are paid, and no stress or worrying about how you are going to keep the lights on or pay rent. This has to be one of the most fulfilling feelings in the world, especially when it is a result of doing the work you love. I believe the real path to gaining financial freedom and living a fulfilling life on your terms is through pushing past fears to do what you love and finding a way to build wealth from it. You might be thinking, "I don't want to be my own boss or be wealthy". It's ok if you feel that way because you have your own dreams. You may even be thinking I'm shallow for focusing on making a lot of money. The truth is, in our society, being wealthy affords you opportunities to experience more of life. It enables you to fund projects and creative ideas that can create jobs and opportunities for others. No matter what you dream, the question is are you pursuing it?

Do you recognize your dreams and pursue them as if your life depends on them? Wealth can be created in several ways. Some of the most effective ways have been by creating content, products, or services that are needed and useful. Look at Steve Jobs, Mark Zuckerberg, Elon Musk, and Mark Cuban. These guys are moguls but they weren't always known as the big names we see them as today. Their creativity, ideas, talent, skills, efforts, experience, persistence, and vision created their golden ticket to financial freedom. Their ability to push past fears while continuing to pursue their dreams helped create their destiny. What about your destiny? Do you feel you are currently on the right path? Is there something nudging you to focus your attention in a certain direction? Your dreams are the vehicle directing you toward your best life. With passion and persistence, you can make your dreams come true but you have to take the first step.

I remember hearing a subtle voice like a whisper saying to me, "There is something else out there for you." This started during a time when I didn't know what I wanted for my life, or know what this "something" was, or why I was hearing those words. It was a quiet subtle voice every time I came home from a stressful day at work. There were days when I felt like I had no clue what to do next with my life and career. I felt defeated. I couldn't identify my passion or the things I did well and enjoyed to make an income. I would often question the reasons for continuing this unfulfilling routine of waking up, driving to work, working eight hours or more, five to seven days a week, then coming home to a feeling of emptiness and discontent. The days were long, and I had no real passion for the type of job I was working. I worked in customer service, retail, and telemarketing, as a video game tester, a supervisor, a help-desk support representative, an office clerk, and a Lyft and Uber driver. They all had one thing in common. I hated every single one of them. No disrespect toward you if you are currently working in any of these professions. I didn't hate them they just weren't what I was passionate about. I am thankful for these experiences because they served a purpose at the time when I needed them most. I appreciate these opportunities as they have all shaped me into the person I am today. Deep down I have always felt a deep sense of purpose to be on a stage in front of an audience instead of at a desk behind a computer. What I noticed about my habits with all of these jobs is that I would work for a company for two years, and then I would be ready to move on to something else. I would master them and be ready for the next challenge or I would feel discontent. Often I would hear that quietly crisp echo in the back of my mind reminding me with every job, "There is something else better out there."

If I wanted to live life on my terms and attempt to become financially free, I had to find what I enjoyed doing for a living. I knew this would require me to take a risk and bet on my potential, and myself but I had little confidence in myself and no idea what I wanted to pursue. After fifteen years of chasing jobs and not chasing my dreams, I finally got sick of working these unfulfilling jobs that were sucking the life out of me. The only logical option I could think of was to become an entrepreneur or entertainer. I felt that was the only way for me to find fulfillment in my life but what I pursued next had to be bigger than me. I looked at the successes of people like Oprah Winfrey, Steve Harvey, Bill Gates, Steve Jobs, LeBron James, Kobe Bryant, Mariah Carey, and hundreds of others who I always wondered, what do they have that I don't?

I compared them to me, the "average" employee, at the time, and I wanted to figure out what our differences were so I could understand what I needed to do to change my life. As I was comparing them, I got a sheet of paper and I drew a line down the middle to create a divide. On the left side, I labeled it "Me," and on the right, I labeled it "Them." Then I would list all the attributes I could name about me and them. For me, I was a good communicator and leader, talented with music, a risk taker, but I lacked discipline, wealth, and self-confidence, and never owned a business. They all shared common attributes such as being self-disciplined, persistent, dedicated, and connected to their talent, risk takers, good communicators, wealthy, confident, entrepreneurs, dream chasers, and effective leaders. After comparing attributes I realized they were not much different from me on paper. The biggest difference was that they chose to pursue dreams and I chose to pursue jobs.

It was during that moment I had finally reached a point in my life where I understood I no longer wanted to be an employee. I wanted to pursue something different. I was almost thirty years old and I still didn't have a clear picture of what my dreams were. I knew I was creative and a risk-taker. I wanted to use my current skills and talents to change directions in my life and career, but I didn't know where to start. I did not have a product to sell or know what services I could offer. By this point in my life, I was already a music producer with hundreds of songs and over fifteen years of experience. My first thought was that I could sell music as a product and sell studio time as a service to other artists. I purchased business cards and created a website. I took time to make a business plan after I found a free template online. I created fliers and began promoting them on social media. It was exciting, but something in my mind kept nagging me and saying, "You're never going to make money doing this." I even kept telling myself it would take too much time to get started or that no one would want to pay me for my music. I doubted my creativity and myself. I continued finding more reasons why I should give up instead of reasons why I should continue. Eventually, I talked myself out of it—just like all the other times I walked away from things I wanted to pursue but allowed fear and doubt to stop me. I continued producing music but walked away from making it a business because of fear.

Another example of allowing fear to control my decisions is when I moved to California in 2002 from Cleveland Ohio to pursue becoming a recording artist and music producer at the age of nineteen. I dropped out of college and moved to Los Angeles with only $250, my suitcase, a pillow, and my Casio keyboard. I had no job, and I was sleeping on the floor in my cousin's dorm room at California State University, Northridge. I was taking courses to study audio engineering so I could learn how to record my music and work in a recording studio. I took a nine-hundred-hour course at the Los Angeles Recording Workshop in North Hollywood. I thought it was cool to be in a professional recording studio to learn the mixing consoles and play with all the instruments and gear. I was a shy kid from Cleveland and an introvert. It was challenging trying to meet new people because I kept to myself in class. I wanted to take my notes, ask any questions I needed help with, and go home. I was not very social around strangers.

When I finished the nine hundred hours of classes, all I had to do to get certified was complete a ninety-day internship at a professional recording studio. I allowed my fears to convince me into believing that I wouldn't be able to find a job after interning, and I continued telling myself all kinds of stories like I wouldn't be successful, this was just a stupid dream, and that I needed a "real" job or I could be homeless. I thought a "real" job meant working behind a desk forty hours a week, five days a week. I didn't take the courses seriously enough because of my fears and I failed because I gave up before I got certified.

Fear held me back and a lack of vision for my career as an audio engineer didn't allow me to see a clear path to becoming successful at it. I knew I loved being in the studio environment as a producer and artist. I also love the art of mixing and the creative process of recording and arranging music. I love the experience, but I did not see myself sitting in a recording studio for ten-plus hours at a time unless I was the artist behind the microphone or the producer behind the keyboard. I needed to earn money fast and that fed my fears. I used to think I was a failure. Looking back on it now, I realize this experience did not make me a failure. It was a necessary part of my journey. A lesson learned.

At the time, I had no clue I would later be forced to revisit this path and that an opportunity would present itself fifteen years later; only to uncover a deeper realization that I never could have imagined. I will come back to this later, but this deeper realization turned out to be one of the most definitive moments of my life so far along my journey.

The lesson I learned about myself after not completing the audio engineering internship and after quitting multiple jobs over the years is that I had a habit of starting things and not following through with them until the end. I was repeating this same pattern of quitting something and not following through with it for several years. When I decided to start my own business and discovered my passion for inspirational speaking, I knew I would have to break the cycle. This realization was the catalyst that has helped me to work on pushing past my fears to pursue my dreams. I was afraid of public speaking, and I had to overcome this fear but I'll explain that later. It was time to start finding answers about my life's purpose. First, I had to start answering tough questions. I would wonder things like, Why am I not happy with myself? What else can I do with my life? What did I need to know? Who did I need to meet? Who did I need to become? I had to write a list of what I felt was important to help me to start the process of figuring things out.

What I learned about myself during this period in my life are some of the things that drive me to want to pursue my dreams and be successful:

1. I want to inspire others.
2. I want to live life on my terms.
3. I want to take care of my family.
4. I want to experience things that will enrich, empower, and transform my life.
5. I want to travel the world and experience more.

What are the five things that drive you to want to be successful along your journey?

Think of five things to list for each category: career, relationships, personal development, finances, and any other areas of your life.

IDENTIFYING YOUR WHY

What drives you to pursue your dreams? Knowing your WHY is one of the most important pieces to pursuing your dreams. I started searching YouTube videos for topics on how to start a business, and I clicked on a video by accident. The video was by motivational speaker Eric Thomas. In the video, he was talking about how important it is to know your why.

Your why is the reason you are doing what you are doing to motivate yourself on days when you don't think you have enough left in you to keep pushing. So I sat down and wrote another list with my why.

Below are some of the reasons why I do what I do every day:

- For my mom, dad, and family
- For my future self

- To inspire the world to pursue their passions and dreams
- For those who think it is impossible to live their dreams
- For those who are afraid to take the first steps to pursue their dreams
- For those who don't believe there is more to life
- For those who need a positive example
- For those who died before accomplishing their dreams
- For those who believe in me
- For those who support my vision
- For those who have taught me something along my journey
- For all of you who are only one thought, idea, or action away from recognizing your full potential
- For those who said it wasn't possible

If you have reached a point in your life where you are tired of your career choices, or feel like your life is heading further away in an opposite direction of what you desire, or you continue to repeat the same emotional cycle filled with discontent in the things you are currently doing, it is time to take a step back and look at your reasons why. Your *why* motivates you. It is your emotional blueprint behind why you do what you do. It is time to take notes!

CHALLENGE #1

For this challenge, take a moment to answer the following questions. You will need to write your answers on a sheet of paper, or you can use your mobile device to take notes. Write down the answers for each question. Be honest, take your time, and be specific.

1. What makes you smile? (activities, people, events, hobbies, projects, etc.)
2. Who inspires you most? (anyone you know or do not know—family, friends, authors, artists, leaders, etc.)
3. What things do you do well and enjoy?
4. What do other people say you are good at doing?
5. What do people typically ask you for help in?
6. If you had to teach something, what would you teach?
7. What would you regret not doing or having in your life?
8. What are your reasons why?

Inspirational Moment with TL

Life is what you make it. The best thing you can do is make your life work for you.

CHAPTER TWO: LIFE WITHOUT A DREAM

I hit a bump in the road when I was twenty-six. I was dealing with being laid off from two jobs in a row and having to decide if I would be able to afford the cost of living in Los Angeles or move back home to Cleveland to stay with my mom until I could get back on my feet. I spoke to my aunt Carolyn for advice before I made my decision. She was a career counselor for UCLA and El Camino College for thirty years and now is an entrepreneur, trainer, and bestselling author of many books, one of which is titled *Life Lessons from the Soul: A Path to Happiness and Success.* I asked her if she thought it was a good idea for me to move back home. I told her I felt going back home would be like taking steps backward because I spent seven years trying to build my life in Los Angeles, but I needed to downsize. If I moved back home, I would have an opportunity to return to college to get a degree. I loved the sunny warm weather, creative atmosphere, and energy in Los Angeles. It was hard to let that experience go to return home to a mostly cold, wet, and often dreary place. It was home and that had been all I experienced until I moved to Los Angeles. I never forgot where I came from; I had just gotten used to being in a different climate.

As we continued the discussion about my concerns about moving back home, she understood them and how I perceived this move as though I was taking steps backward. She insisted that I not see it as taking steps backward. She told me to see it as if I were taking steps forward in a new direction. She said, "Sometimes you have to take steps that feel like a step backward, to position yourself to take two steps ahead." I remember thinking, "That's easier said than done." I felt like I was packing up my manhood to go back to being dependent on my mother to take care of me as a twenty-six-year-old grown man. I had to put my pride aside to see her positive spin on how I could view things. Deep down I knew she was right.

Reflective moment:

1. Have you ever had a life event happen to you that pushed you into having to make a life-altering decision?
2. What are some fears you experienced before and after making your life-altering decision?
3. What was the outcome?
4. How have you changed as a result of making your life-altering decision? Has it made you a stronger person?

My aunt stressed that no matter what decision I made, it was very important I never lose sight of the reasons why I decided to move to California in the first place. She said, "There is something that pulled you to live in California." She continued, "If you have a dream, you must honor it." She said, "I remember when you were fifteen years old and you told me you wanted to be successful in music. You said that one day you were going to live in Los Angeles. Then, four years later you turned that into a reality." Then she stressed the point: "Please never lose sight of that. Make sure you weigh the pros and cons of both staying in California and moving back to Cleveland before you make a decision."

I took her advice. My pros for staying in Los Angeles were that I loved the weather, the beaches, the atmosphere, and being close to the entertainment industry. The cons were that it was expensive to live there and I was unemployed. The pros for moving back to Cleveland were that I would be able to spend more time with my mother and family, and I would be able to attend college without having to worry about the expenses of rent. The cons were that I would have to deal with the cold, snowy winters and not be able to go to the beach. Not too many cons, as you can see. I chose to return home, but I made a promise to myself that I would return to Los Angeles in four years. After returning home, I earned a degree in information technology, graduated summa cum laude, and returned to Los Angeles within three years. I was determined to stick to my plan.

CHALLENGE #2

For this challenge, you will need to write your answers on a sheet of paper, or you can use your mobile device to take notes. Write down the answers to the question below. Be honest, take your time, and be specific. What are the pros and cons of pursuing your dream?

You can split this into two separate columns so you can have a side-by-side visual. Label one side "Pros" and the other side "Cons."

PROS   **CONS**

Inspirational Moment with TL

When life knocks you down, fight back and claim your victory. Never back down; always stand up.

CHAPTER THREE: THE DREAMLESS ZOMBIE

When you give up on your dreams, you start to lose a sense of who you are. You will find that you often compare yourself with other people who are successful in following their dreams and you start to believe that they are special or elite. You become sad and depressed because of the empty hole eating away at the inner core of your existence stretching outward as it completely takes over like a thief in dark clothing who ran away with your soul. The difference between those who are successfully living their dreams and those who are stuck living in fear is that one of those groups pushed past their fears and the other one didn't.

The fears of failure, change, not being good enough, the unknown, judgment, and rejection can make you want to give up and stop pursuing your dreams before you even take the first step. Your fears are tricky and will influence you to rationalize your lack of taking action to convince you that no action is the right action. You will never see proof of progress if you don't take action. If you stop taking action or never take action at all, your momentum will fade, your dream will fade, and a part of you will fade. When you stop dreaming, you stop learning. When you stop learning, you stop hoping. When you stop hoping, you stop reaching, and when you stop reaching, you stop living. You may not die, but if you turned on the light in your mind, you'd probably see that no one was home.

Have you ever seen the hit television show on AMC called *The Walking Dead*? When you lose sight of your dreams and stop living life with a purpose, you start roaming around like a zombie. Instead of searching for blood and flesh, you are searching for something outside of you to save you. You want this external source, person, thing, or event to come to save you from your fears and force you to take action to pursue your dreams.

As the dreamless zombie, you focus on individuals whom you view as being more successful than you. You cast judgment on them and resent them because they are living their dreams, while you are feeling sorry for yourself as if life has been unfair only to you. You have somehow convinced yourself that life has been so unreasonable because you weren't born as one of the "special lucky ones" who get to be successful and live their dreams while you are feeling sorry for yourself. You hate yourself and it is hard to look at yourself in the mirror to face the person you've become while wanting to see the person you wish you could be. You lash out in anger against the world instead of taking a deeper look within to see the only thing stopping you is *you*. This is life without pursuing a dream. Stop comparing what everyone else has achieved and beating yourself up over it.

The only thing stopping you from getting from where you are to where you want to be is *you*. You can change that at any given moment. Decide right now to only concern yourself with finding the real you and the dream you have in your heart. Start working toward those things. Test your limits and push yourself past the fears that have been holding you back from pursuing your dream.

There is no need to be concerned with what others have because what they have is for them. You possess the same power and control over your mind and how you respond to your fears. You could have so much more if you choose to believe it is possible for you. You don't have to be someone else. Understand it is OK to be you. You have your own expression and will make your contribution to the world. Think about who you are, what it is you love doing, make a plan, and work hard doing a little bit at a time every day. Believe in the endless possibilities life has to offer. You must pursue your passions and work on your dreams with a sense of urgency. You have to stand up within yourself to demand control of your mind and your circumstances. Don't be a dreamless zombie. Life doesn't happen to you; you create your life.

Reflective moment:

1. How many dreamless zombies do you know in your life?
2. Are you the dreamless zombie? If so, what actions toward pursuing your dream can you take to bring more life into it?
3. What beliefs have you been holding on to that have been preventing you from taking action?

Inspirational Moment with TL

Change is the first step from who you are to who you will become.

OUTSIDE OF YOUR ZONE

Discovering your dreams is an inside job and requires you to step outside of your comfort zone. You will be amazed by the lessons you learn about yourself and your potential when you step outside of your comfort zone. It all starts with you. One of the most important missions in life is to find your truest expression and what you are born to do. This raw expression of who you are is attached to your dream. To discover what you are born to do, you have to live outside your comfort zone. Steve Harvey once said, "There are two most important days in your life. The day you are born and the day you discover why." You will discover the higher meaning of why you were born if you are willing to work on yourself, push past your fears, and take action to discover yourself.

For some, this will happen naturally. For others like myself, it takes being forced by frustration, discontent, and feeling like there is no other way but to move forward on your dream before we reach the point when we start following the whispering voice saying, "There is something else better out there." Yet some discover themselves and have a dream they want to pursue, but because of fear, they never take the first step. What if Oprah Winfrey and Tyler Perry never pursued their dreams? How would the entertainment industry be? What if Michael Jackson never pursued his dream? What if Barack Obama never pursued his dream? What if Martin Luther King Jr. never shared his dream?

These highly influential people are living proof of what is possible when you step outside of your comfort zone to pursue your dreams. So how do you get there? Do you think Will Smith was afraid of something when he did his first acting audition? Do you think Ellen DeGeneres was afraid of something when she aired her first TV episode? Of course! They were all afraid of something. The difference between them and the people who allow their fears to become permanent barriers is a simple fact that they felt the fear and did it anyway. As we focus more on fears, we create more limits to what we view as possible. The barriers we create in our minds keep us in our comfort zone.

When you are afraid of something, it is easy to downplay your ability. You write off your dreams before ever starting because you don't think you are good enough, smart enough, or capable to handle the failure or success of your dream. You may also get discouraged because of the time it will take to achieve your goals. Fear makes you feel like a victim and it holds you back making you believe there is nothing you can do about it. Some people think you have to have years of experience or have to be perfect at something to start pursuing a dream. They allow the fear of making mistakes to prevent them from taking the first step. The good news is you don't have to be perfect to get started with your dream! It is foolish to think that you will not make mistakes with something you've never done. There is learning and preparation involved in pursuing your dreams. The experience of growth happens as a result of taking action. Remember it is not your dream that has to be prepared; it is you that must be prepared for your dream. The journey is a marathon, not a sprint. Be patient and allow yourself to enjoy the experience. You have to act on your dreams and it starts right now.

CHALLENGE #3

Stepping outside of your comfort zone can be fun, and it can teach you more things about yourself that you weren't aware of. Your challenge for the next seven days is to do everyday things differently. Take a different route to work, wake up earlier than usual to get a head start on your morning, eat breakfast for dinner and dinner for breakfast, or try a new hobby. The whole point is to do something outside of your normal daily routine to push yourself outside of your comfort zone.

Next, I want you to share your experience by joining my Facebook group page called "Dreamer's Journey" (www.facebook.com/groups/dreamersjourney).

Inspirational Moment with TL

You see, therefore you think. As you think, you begin to feel. As you feel, you begin to act. As a result, you can live your dreams even if all you have afterward is faith and a purpose.

CHAPTER FOUR: A NEW CHAPTER

In July 2012, I had over $8,000 in my savings account. After three years of staying with my mom, I had saved up enough money, and I was right on track with my goal of moving back to California. I had a plan in place to temporarily stay with my cousin again; this time I would be sleeping on the floor in his studio bedroom apartment. My car was packed from door to door. I packed up everything I could fit into my two-door gray Honda Accord and hit the road with my father who has always been there to help me with my cross-country moves. Since he lived in another state, our road trips were exciting because they gave us a chance to spend time together.

Our favorite road song to keep us energized during the two-thousand-mile road trip was "Roses," by OutKast. I was surprised my dad liked this song, but every time it would play on my mix CD, he would start dancing in his seat. We played it several times throughout the trip and had a blast together. The drive was long. It was summer, so it was very hot. We had to drive cross-country twice, and each time it took us three days, but it was a fun experience we will never forget. I was determined to come back to Los Angeles stronger, smarter, and better than I was when I left back in 2009. I was looking forward to what the future had in store for me.

We were singing songs together and talking about life and bonding with each other during the trip. It was also nice to see all of the trees and landscapes from the different states we passed by. We took the southern route on the 40 West interstate freeway. We drove through nine states: Ohio, Indiana, Illinois, Missouri, Oklahoma, Texas, New Mexico, Arizona, and California. It was the second-longest trip ever, but it was worth the experience.

When I arrived in Los Angeles after moving from Ohio for the second time, I was filled with happiness and gratitude for my achievement. I was excited to be back. The first couple of weeks I was trying to do it all. I took trips to the beach every day for a week, I was dating again after a two-year hiatus, and I was temporarily experiencing pure freedom without working a job while living off my savings until I found my next job. I wanted to enjoy as much of this freedom as I could because reality would eventually catch up with me. After six months, I began to run out of money. It was time to get serious.

I wanted to avoid being in the same position again where I needed to find a job as soon as possible to start making an income. I got all the way down to about $2,000, and the internal red alarm was beginning to go off in my mind. It was time to start working before I depleted my savings. I was sleeping on couches, floors, and even in my car at times. I was ready for change and needed to make something happen. I finally landed a temporary job with a packaging company working part-time. At the time, I was so focused on trying to get a full-time job because I wanted to be able to afford the rent for my first one-bedroom apartment by myself. I had been waiting so impatiently to have my own place to live for the past four years, but I was only working part-time and needed to earn more money. After work, I would take a trip over to the beach to collect my thoughts. I would spend a few hours watching the waves crash against the shore, as I listened to the peaceful sounds of the Pacific Ocean. I would sit on the sand looking out into the distance of what appeared to be an endless body of water while thinking about my life and trying to understand what I was passionate about pursuing as a career. I enjoyed watching the sunset. As I was sitting in the sand, I was thinking about how I wanted something that would bring more joy and happiness in my life that I could earn a living from. I wanted a profession, not a job. If I am going to wake up every morning to spend several hours of my time, it better be with something I enjoy.

Even though I had a degree in information technology, that wasn't a passion for me. I chose this degree because I wanted a well-paying job, and I saw a possibility for sustainable employment in the technology industry. I figured technology would always be around. I wanted to set myself up to always have something to fall back on. As if I didn't learn my lesson about job security three years ago when I got laid off.

During those times I spent going to the beach after work, I recorded my thoughts on a voice memo app on my phone. I would have conversations on the beach with nothing other than my recorder rolling. I'd talk about life and what all it meant. I would "people watch" and try to understand how we are all connected with each other and the universe.

I would ask for guidance, a better understanding, and for the ability to see a better way of living that utilizes my skills and passions. I didn't know it at the time; but four years later, I would discover, I was recording the very content you are reading now.

After eight months of job searching, I finally received a call for an interview for a technology help-desk support position with a big entertainment company in Glendale, California. The interview was on a hot summer day in August 2012. I was confident but nervous. I went into the interview, and there was a panel of six people watching me like a hawk. I kept my cool and went along with the interview, but it only lasted fifteen minutes. That seemed to be a little bit short, but I had answered all the questions well and I just felt like I aced that interview like a pro. I knew it would only be a couple of days before I would get their phone call telling me to report to my new job. I sent a thank-you e-mail the next day and waited for a week, but I never received a response. Wait, what?

A week went by and no response. Now I was concerned. I sent a follow-up e-mail to find out if they had reached a decision. To my surprise, I received a response later in the day. Their response was, "Thank you for interviewing with us. We believe you have the skills and experience we are looking for but unfortunately, we decided to go with another candidate who is a little more qualified for the position. We will keep your resume on file for future consideration."

For the first few seconds after reading that e-mail, I felt defeated, but something inside of me said, "You came this far; don't be discouraged." Deep down I knew that that voice was right. I couldn't let something like this tear me down. I remember thinking,

"This must not be meant for me." I had to find another way to survive because I knew in situations like this; the worst thing I could do is think negatively. I stayed positive and kept looking.

Reflective moment:

1. How many times in your life have you been disappointed by something you wanted?
2. Do you tend to think of all the negative things causing your disappointment, or do you try to find the positives?
3. If something doesn't happen the way you expect it to, do you think of that as a bad thing, or do you think of this as a learning opportunity?

I had to let my disappointment go, and I wrote it off as a learning experience. I learned I could handle a panel of six people drilling me for fifteen minutes I guess. I needed to focus my attention in another direction, so I started looking for my next full-time job.

I contacted friends and associates to ask about job opportunities, and no one had any leads. I was searching all over the Internet for job listings. For most of the jobs I applied for I would get replies saying either I was "overqualified" or "not what we are looking for at this time." I could understand if I was not what they were looking for, but "overqualified"…really? I'm not too sure why that is a bad thing for any job candidate, but I didn't have time to dwell on it. I continued working on staying positive and visualizing my goals. Before I knew it, I was working a full-time job of applying for jobs all day long. The benefits sucked, and the pay was crappy. Oh yeah, I'm supposed to be positive huh?

Five months later, the employer whom I had interviewed with in August contacted me. They asked me to come in for a second interview. I was so shocked they contacted me and so excited I could barely contain my excitement over the phone. I was invited back for a second interview, and I was offered the job as a temporary employee with a thirty-day trial period. A good friend allowed me to sleep on his couch for a few weeks until I could save up enough money to move into an apartment. At this point, one of my problems was solved. I got a full-time job. However, the thirty-day temporary-employee status threw things off. At least I would be able to make money during that period to pay bills, so that problem was also solved, but I still needed to work on getting off my friend's couch. I did the best I could to show my boss I was a good choice so that he would hire me full-time.

I had to prove to myself I could handle this new job and prove to my boss that I was good enough to be hired full-time. I decided to put pressure on myself so that I had no choice but to do a great job. I made a bold move after two weeks into my thirty-day trial period as a temporary employee. I was tired of sleeping on couches and floors, so I signed a one-year lease for a one-bedroom apartment before I was offered the full-time position. I guess I said to myself if the law of attraction is really what they say it is, then now is a good time for it to prove itself.

When I signed the lease to my apartment and committed to it, I had no choice but to accept the circumstances and trust in my ability to do well in my new job. I went to work the next day, looked my boss right in the eyes, and said, "Thank you for this opportunity. You made a great choice. I just want you to know that I will work hard for you, and I will be successful in my role." From that point forward, I never looked back or regretted my decision to move my life forward even during a time of uncertainty.

In less than a month on the job, I became a regular full-time employee with benefits, and I was making the highest-paid salary I had ever been offered in my life at that time. I learned from this and many other experiences that the law of attraction is real. What you focus on, you create. The key ingredients are taking action and believing. By taking action, you push what you focus on into existence and the universe works to support you. By believing, you confirm that what you are pursuing is already yours. Everything worked out just fine. I was finally starting to see the light at the end of the tunnel.

Reflective moment:

1. What risks are you willing to take to get what you want?
2. Do you believe you create things in your life based on your combination of focus and taking action?
3. How will you know when a risk is worth taking?

Inspirational Moment with TL
Your dreams **can** *become reality. Your dreams* **will** *become reality.*
Your dreams **are** *reality. Think it, and you will become it.*

OUTSIDE OF THE FOUR WALLS

I finally reached two major goals. I had a full-time job with income coming in, and I was able to support myself without needing help from my parents. Yes, when you live in Los Angeles, it is a major accomplishment to be able to afford to live by yourself. I was feeling very grateful. It was a big accomplishment and a testament to how faith and persistence produced results.

I was happy to be working again, and I was thankful for how things just fell into place. I reported to work and as I was about to enter the building on my first day, something interesting happened. That quiet voice in the background kept whispering, "This is only temporary. There is still something else better out there." I didn't know what that something else was at the time, so I continued with my first day at my new job. The first day on the job I noticed a huge red flag from the first few minutes after walking in the door. It was like an alarm going off in my mind, and my only response was "What the hell did I just get myself into?" Before getting instructions on what I needed to do in my new role as a technology help-desk support representative, I was greeted by my new boss who was going off on my coworker about not refilling the paper trays in the printer. He seemed to be very adamant about it for some reason. He had his printer in his office, but for some reason, he was concerned about ours.

Being the new guy, I wasn't sure what the big deal was, but perhaps the printer was an important tool for our department. I just sat back and listened so I could understand why he was upset. He acted as if not refilling the paper trays immediately after running out of paper would cause the entire business to shut down for the day.

I tried to think nothing of it and just focused on learning my job. My first impression of this guy was that he seemed to be very strict with the way he ran his department. As the days went on, there were more incidents where I witnessed his temper and reactiveness to often minor things. I guess because I was new, he directed most of his temper and smart remarks toward my coworker. As an outsider, it seemed to me that he would always target my coworker with his sarcasm and temper. I think it was because he may have felt my coworker was a good punching bag for his frustrations.

My coworker was a quiet and shy kind of guy who did the best he could but often fell short of meeting the boss's expectations. I believe he felt intimidated by our boss, and our boss could smell that a mile away so he used that to his advantage. I mean, we did work directly under a vice president of a department, so that alone could make anyone feel like you have to be on top of your game. It also didn't help that his office was right next to our cubicle. He would often pop up at our desk, so we had to make sure we were always "on the lookout." One day my coworker made a few mistakes on an Excel report we had to share with our boss to track some items for the department, and my boss got so angry at my coworker.

I remember he came storming over to our desk and approached my coworker as if he was about to have a nervous breakdown. He was upset because of the mistake made on the report and said to him, "Are you trying to destroy me and everything I have done in the past twelve years?"

I was thinking to myself, "Damn, it's only a few columns that aren't titled correctly; it's not the end of your career here."

He would blow the littlest things out of proportion. I had heard stories about this guy from some of the people in the department who had been dealing with his emotionally charged behavior for many years. Somehow they managed to suck it up and deal with it. I could tell early on that I was not going to be one of them. I witnessed his sarcastic comments and unpredictable attitude many days working for him. I think my biggest issue with this guy was that he would never smile unless he was talking about himself or being sarcastic. Deep down he had to be a good person, but in his role as the head of the department, he was a piece of work.

His energy was intense, and every day it felt like we were walking on eggshells to bypass him. He was like a walking heart attack waiting to happen. It appeared as though he was under a lot of stress and was unhappy about something in his life, which often caused him to overreact. I could understand if he was stressed or felt a sense of entitlement because he was the head of the department. He worked hard to get where he was and I respected that. I had to frequently stop and ask myself what the hell did I just get myself into. The hardest part to admit to myself at the time was that I believed this was the only way I could make money to pay rent, so I stuck with the job for over two years. Deep down I knew there was something else better out there for me. The voice I heard in my head on the first day was right. It was time for me to get my values in check and come up with a better approach to my life and career.

In the meantime, I needed to do what I had to do to stay off the streets, so I chose to deal with it to make it work. Besides, the job was paying over $50,000 a year, so it wasn't too hard to be a yes-man for a short period until I figured my life out. Aside from dealing with an overreactive boss every day, my job became manageable. I learned some very valuable lessons from it that would later cause a paradigm shift in the way I approached my life.

If you have ever worked for or with someone who needs to control, it keeps you on your toes. It was at this job that I developed the skill of high-volume multitasking, time management, and heavy workload balance. It was like a circus juggling act. As a help-desk support representative for over five hundred users, I had several hours of practice with answering phones and listening to users report their issues while at the same time taking notes, dealing with people approaching my desk to ask questions, and assisting with ordering and receiving equipment. Often all this was happening at once. So when something slipped through the cracks, it's no wonder why management would freak out. I mean it's not like we had enough going on already right?

I remember the question what am I doing here kept coming to mind while I was working there. It seemed like the more I searched for the answer, the more I started wondering about everyone else around me, including my boss. What are they doing here? As I was seeking to understand the answer to this question for myself, I also decided to shift gears to focus on the lessons I needed to learn from this experience. The questions I asked myself next were, what can I learn from this experience, and what can I learn from my boss about being a leader? When you are dealing with an undesirable situation, you will drive yourself mad if you focus on the negative aspects of the situation. In every difficult or undesirable situation, it's important to uncover the lesson behind it.

I started to pay more attention to my boss to understand who he was and why he reacted so aggressively to things. I kind of felt like maybe I could help in some kind of way or at the very least, learn what not to do as a leader by watching him. What I learned about him was shocking. What I learned from him shifted my focus for the rest of my life.

An opportunity to understand my boss came during our first private lunch meeting I was required to have with him once a year. The purpose of the meeting was so we could get to know more about each other to discuss progress and goals for our department.

We started talking about family and what led us to the company. I asked him, "Have you ever had a dream of becoming your own boss?" He said, "Yes, a long time ago when I was in college." I said, "I'm not surprised, you are very intelligent, and I can see you developing a new software or running your own business, kind of like the next Bill Gates." He laughed and seemed flattered by my comment. He said, "That's interesting because I created a software program years ago, but I kept running into roadblocks trying to get it into the right hands, so I eventually gave it up." He continued to say, "During my first marriage, I started my career in the technology industry over twenty years ago and when I started with this company, I started focusing more on my job."

To my surprise, he then leaned over to me and said, "I'm going to let you in on a little secret; don't repeat this." He said, "There has been so much work that has come across my desk over the past few months, which has become very overwhelming. I know you guys probably see me wound up and overreacting to things, but I have to tell you this job is very stressful. I'm talking, like, foaming-at-the-mouth, give-me-ulcers type of stress. So that is a small glimpse into what I've been dealing with for several months."

I was shocked to hear his candid disclosure about his feelings and what he was experiencing. For the first time, he was communicating with me as if I was a friend instead of someone who reported to him. I asked him, "How come you haven't returned to software development?" He said, "Becoming a software developer was never my dream. It was my dad's dream and ever since I decided to go a different direction with my career, he stopped speaking to me as if I wasn't good enough or as if I disobeyed his wishes." I asked him, so why not pursue something you are passionate about instead? He replied, "Because I'm not sure what that is. I proved to myself that I could be successful, but there is something else out there for me. I just haven't found what that is." He continued to say, "I also would like to fix the relationship I have with my father."

What shocked me most is that I was sitting next to this high-level department head with years of experience. He was a technology genius who prided himself on his hard work, knowledge, and status. He was well known but least favored because of his personality and communication style with others. Yet deep down inside his core, he was dealing with the effects of living in a constant state of pressure in his career, rejection from his father, a failed marriage, and a lack of fulfillment and purpose in his life. I was starting to connect the dots into who he was as a real person and not just as an authority figure.

I was beginning to understand why he was reacting to things so aggressively, and my perspective of him completely changed. He had been misdirecting years of frustration, stress, and discontent because of the things that he had been dealing with for many years of his life. It was during this moment I realized this person who came across as overreactive and sarcastic isn't as bad as he appeared on the outside. He was broken on the inside, and I wanted to help him, but I knew I wouldn't be able to. All I could do was learn from him instead. His approach to leadership was based on spreading fear and control to get what he needed out of his team.

I learned that great leaders inspire their teams: they don't intimidate or use fear. I learned that your words and actions have power and the way you communicate with others has an impact. How could I allow someone who wasn't a great leader to tell me what I should do? He was just another human being trying to get through life the best way he knows how while dealing with his circumstances and a stressful job. Once I came to this realization, it was time to reassess my next career move. I was unhappy working for this person, and the job was not a passion of mine. The person I was working for, his leadership style, his behavior, and his attitude were confirmations that I had to do something else for my future. I learned a very valuable lesson that created a shift in my life and what I valued. After our lunch meeting, I felt a sense of closure in this situation of dealing with him and my job. I made a promise to myself that I will never put myself in a situation where I had to work for anyone like him again.

It is because of this experience I learned the true way to fulfillment is to follow your passion and create a way to get paid doing what you love so you can be your own boss. I wanted to be free and be my own boss. It was time to work on figuring out how to make that happen.

I was feeling discontent with the work I was doing. I got tired of dealing with things that didn't matter. I was dealing with people complaining about their computers. I had to defend myself against different personalities of people who felt entitled because of their job titles. I felt like it was all nonsense. I was starting to see through the delusion that my boss and most of us operated under as employees. Just because you run a department does not mean you are "special" or that you can treat people poorly. You have a job title with a specific responsibility and duty to serve the company. If you are a good leader, you lead your team most effectively by building them up, not by tearing them down and manipulating them by using fear or intimidation. They depend on your guidance and support. Most employees want to go to work, perform to the best of their abilities, and feel supported by their leaders. If you don't invest in making your team better by inspiring them to be their best and encouraging their efforts you, put the success of the team in jeopardy.

Once you step outside of the four walls of the office, you are just an average Joe. Your job title means absolutely nothing outside of the building you work. So the delusion of being "entitled" or being "important" because of your job title is only valid inside the four walls of your job. It was crazy to hear people on the team complain about him and the department but not do anything about it to change it. Most of them would suck it up and deal with it. I was not going to be one of them.

This job had served its purpose, and it was time to move on. I was thankful for the opportunity at the moment I needed the opportunity. I was grateful to have a source of income, especially after what I had been through trying to get the job but I wasn't happy with the direction my life was heading. I was spending forty hours or more a week at work. I was around my coworkers more than my family. I was missing out on beautiful sunny days and trips to the beach because I was stuck behind the four walls of the cubicle cage. I was missing out on life. I wasn't saving lives or making anyone else's life or my life better. The job was stressful. I was dealing with over five hundred personalities, a crazy ass boss, solving problems that didn't matter, and forcing myself to care about all of it. It would be insane to realize this and continue putting yourself through it.

All I had been doing was repeating the cycle of "I need to make money to pay bills, so I will find any decent job I can tolerate, to possibly try to move into a higher paying position after a few years, just because it's easier than pursuing my dreams." That was a mouthful but does that sound familiar to you? Have you said something like this before?

It was no longer about just making money. My future and sanity were at stake. I needed to avoid working unfulfilling jobs and begin to chase after more meaningful work that contributes to society on a deeper level. I wanted to experience more of life outside of the four walls of my cubicle.

Reflective moment:

1. How much of life do you get to experience on a day-to-day basis?
2. Have you ever felt like there is more to experience in life than what you have so far?
3. What prevents you from experiencing more in your life?

Inspirational Moment with TL

The moment you focus on what you want, the more you attract what you need.

CHAPTER FIVE: BREAKING OUT OF THE SHELL

I started searching keywords "finding your passion," "motivation," and "self-help" on YouTube one day. I eventually discovered a video by motivational speaker Les Brown. As I watched his videos, I noticed I was feeling motivated. Sounds so obvious but I never heard a motivational speech before so it was working. The more I watched, the more I felt his power as a speaker. I thought it was inspiring to watch this great speaker. He is like everyone else who has had a lot of ups and downs in life, but he shares his stories and uses the public-speaking platform to inspire the world.

I started reflecting on my own story between the ages of nineteen to thirty. I moved from a small suburb named Bedford Heights outside of Cleveland, Ohio, to Los Angeles on my own at the age of nineteen. I built my life from the ground up. I made a lot of bold moves, I've taken a lot of risks, and I've made a lot of sacrifices. I gave up cable and stopped watching TV. You might be thinking, "Big deal—so what that you gave up cable." I did it because it was a distraction. All of that to say, I was dealing with all of these changes while I was simultaneously dealing with my fears. I was dealing with not knowing if I would run out of money. I was dealing with the fear of having to move back to Cleveland for good if this didn't work. I was dealing with not knowing who I was and what I wanted to do with my life. I was dealing with the fear of not figuring out what I was born to do.

Looking back, I believe the one thing that got me from where I was to where I am now is the fact I took action even though I was afraid of not knowing the outcome. I wondered if I could make an impact on the world with my story in such a way that could inspire the world like Les Brown can do. I wonder since he had this type of impact on me, who could I impact?

The challenge I had to face was my fear of public speaking. I would need to be able to speak in front of an audience. It's not rocket science, but I was the type of person who couldn't stand up to speak in a room full of two people, not to mention a room full of thousands, so I questioned if I could do it. I was terrified thinking about having to speak in front of people. I remembered the speech class I was forced to take in college to graduate.

When it was time to prepare and deliver my first speech, I was so afraid I almost passed out from hyperventilating right before I approached the lectern. I had no choice but to do it since it was a requirement. I was so afraid it made me think twice about graduating —that's how painful it was standing in front of people while I presented my speech. It was an icebreaker speech where I had to talk about myself, which made things more difficult. When it was time to speak to the audience, the first words out of my mouth came out with a stutter, as if I had no idea what to say. Even my words were thinking, "Oh hell no, we aren't doing this today." For the next several speeches, I experienced anxiety. I could feel the tension in my throat and the tightness in my stomach each time I would speak. I often found it difficult to remember sections of my speech without messing up because I was so nervous.

One day after my speech class, I came across an advertisement about public speaking training online. I clicked on one link, and then, a series of web pages later, I found myself researching the career paths of public speakers. What I found was that I could use my communication skills to make a great living for myself but I was scared to death of public speaking, so I didn't think much of it.

Twelve years removed from the nineteen-year-old boy I used to be, I was now staring down the path of potentially becoming a public speaker. I ran into an old friend. I mentioned I was thinking about becoming an inspirational speaker and he asked, "Are you going to join Toastmasters?"

I replied, "Toast who? What is that?"

He explained it is an organization for public speakers to help you develop your communication and leadership skills. I didn't know anything about it, but I didn't hesitate to explore it.

I attended my first meeting and fear came with me. I was around a new crowd of people, and I was hoping no one would ask me to speak. I just wanted to observe the meeting. I was not expecting to have to speak, but then they did this thing called a Table Topic. It's an exercise where you are given a random topic to speak extemporaneously for one to two minutes. As soon as I found this out, I was looking for the closest exit.

I believe my fear of public speaking came from when I was in middle school. I was teased all through middle school and high school about the way I talked. My peers would say that I talked " too proper," so I was self-conscious of that when speaking in front of people. For several years, I closed myself into a shell. So when the table topics master called on me to speak, I was nervous, but something in me said to "give it a shot." I couldn't keep running from this fear forever. I stepped to the lectern and gave my best answer. What I love about my Toastmasters experience is that the members are encouraging and supportive. I decided to become a member within the first few visits. This decision changed my life.

After a couple of weeks as a Toastmasters member, I started writing speeches, but I would often find myself at a loss for words. I didn't know what to talk about. I would become frustrated and start doubting my ability to be a speaker. Just as I overcame one obstacle, there was another.

Next, I had to find what I wanted my message to be and figure out how I could use my story to help inspire others. I asked myself, what do people need to hear? I had to start figuring out how to find and communicate my message. What I learned from Les Brown is that many people just like myself need motivation to push them to pursue their dreams. So the next question I needed to answer was, what is stopping you from pursuing your dream? I didn't have an immediate answer. I went into my bedroom and sat at the edge of my bed. I grabbed my phone to record my thoughts. After I finished recording, I started going through my old voice memos of all my other conversations during those times at the beach after I moved back to California two years prior. Then a light bulb went off in my mind. I realized I could use my recorded thoughts to help me work on my speeches and identify the message I wanted to share with the world. It was as if I had been setting myself up for starting my career as an inspirational speaker and author before I ever saw myself pursuing those things. It was meant to be. I was starting to push past a huge fear of public speaking.

I continued practicing speaking. I was signing up to do speeches every week. I also joined multiple clubs to get as much practice in front of an audience as I could. I volunteered to speak during demo meetings to prospective companies who were interested in implementing Toastmasters meetings for their organizations. I competed in multiple speech contests and won multiple first-place awards. I became an award-winning speaker in less than a year. I was improving my communication skills and connecting with more people. I discovered my gift. After some of my speeches, people in the audience would share how my talks inspired them to want to pursue their dreams. People would come up to me to say I seemed very relaxed and that I was a dynamic speaker.

I remember a lady named Gina who had a great big Kool-Aid smile while talking to me after my speech titled Pick up Your Dream. She told me that my speech inspired her. She said she had been running away from her dream for fifteen years. She wanted to be an entrepreneur and start a real-estate business. She said to me, "Your speech opened my eyes to how afraid I am of failing at running my own business." She continued to say, "I realize I have been putting off starting my real-estate business and your speech makes me want to pick my dream back up." This was confirmation that I was going in the right direction. I was starting to make an impact similar to those speakers who inspired me from their YouTube videos. This was all happening because I had a dream and decided to take action.

Reflective moment:

1. What is it that stops most people from pursuing their dreams?
2. What could be preventing you from pursuing a dream or a goal you have always wanted to accomplish?
3. What can you do right now to start working toward that dream?

Inspirational Moment with TL
The sky is the limit. It is time to take off and fly.

CHAPTER SIX: THE SKY IS THE LIMIT

You can create your life into what you want it to be. I wanted to believe this to be true for my life like it appeared to be for all of those highly successful people I mentioned earlier. Again, the one thing they did differently from most people, was to decide to pursue their dreams. When you decide to deliberately take your life into your own hands, you become a conscious creator. The root cause preventing most people from successfully achieving their dreams is their limitations due to fears. They create a huge fence around their potential, like a fence around a private farm. Outside the fence is their dream of what they want to be. Since their past and present don't reflect their dream, they settle for remaining inside the secure farm. Life will give you a preview of what is possible if you pay attention to the signs. Your dream is a sign that you must go beyond the fences of your past and your present to see what is in store for you.

If I was going to help others push past fears to pursue their dreams, I had to help myself first. This required more than just telling people to pick up their dreams. I could potentially impact millions of lives. The only way I could do that is if I practiced what I preached. I was tired of dealing with my demanding boss and years of struggling to understand my purpose. I was tired of unfulfilling jobs taking forty hours of my life away each week. I was tired of feeling like I had so much potential and not doing anything about it. I was getting older and the pressure was there to make something out of my life. I forced myself into a corner and the only way through it was to fight past my fears and doubts.

I revisited my interest in becoming an entrepreneur. Instead of creating a business in the music industry, I decided I would create a business in the personal development industry. I sat down one day and spent several hours mapping out my plans for the business. I started brainstorming ideas for a business name and researched how to start a business and all the expenses I would need to pay. It was kind of fun. I was learning and working on building something from the ground up. I knew I had a lot to learn so I tried to be patient with myself, but that didn't always work because I've always been a little impatient at times. When I have my mind set on something, I want it. Not later, but right now. Call it the only-child syndrome if you want. It's a blessing and a curse at the same time because I drive myself crazy but I produce results.

I wanted things to happen right now. I quickly found out that this expectation was not only ridiculous but also hazardous to my emotional and psychological health. So many of us want everything now. We can't seem to wait for anything anymore. You see this on the roads with impatient drivers, you see this in the grocery stores where people get angry when they have to wait in line, we see this at the airport when flights get delayed, or we see it when things don't turn out the way we want. We get impatient and angry over things that are outside of our control. Some people even throw temper tantrums when things don't go the way they expect. The worse sight to see is a grown person acting like a whiny brat who didn't get to play with his rubber ducky. I digress.

One day while I was on my laptop surfing the web, I came across another YouTube video. This time it was a video by Steve Harvey. In the video, he uses a metaphor in which he says, "If you want to be successful, the thing you have to do is jump." He says, "Every successful person has jumped. You have to take a leap of faith and jump out there as far as you can." It is interesting how much of a role timing plays along your journey. It may sound crazy, but I felt like he was directing his message to me at that moment. It came at the perfect time. I was discovering my passion, and a new vision of my life had begun to form in my mind. I was in the middle of planning a major change in my life. I watched his "jump" video every single day while I was working to keep me motivated and to remind me that there has to be truth in what he was saying. He's living proof of what he is saying you have to do to be successful. I took it to heart and decided to jump.

I have a lot of respect for Steve Harvey. He is a good person with a big heart and great character, and he is in tune with his passion and his purpose. He is a great role model. He often shares his stories of how he became famous and what he went through to be successful. He always inspires his audiences to pursue their gifts. One time I got a chance to catch a live taping of his show *Little Big Shots*. At the end of his show, I remember he said to his audience, "God is in the make-your-dreams-come-true business." He tells his audience, "If you have faith, you cannot let anybody stop you from living your dreams."

In July 2014, I established Dream2Inspire LLC, and my first business was born. I crossed over from wanting to be an employee and not pursuing my dream to becoming my own boss who is now pursuing his dreams and inspiring others to do the same. From this point forward, I had to believe the sky was the limit, and it was time to take off and fly. I'll never forget the day I signed the paperwork to send to the secretary of state to register my business. I was excited but nervous at the same time. After I sealed the envelope with the registration form and check enclosed, I started crying. I was overwhelmed with emotion that I had just created something that could potentially help so many people in the world.

I had some reservations about my decision, mostly due to fear, but I stuck with my plan. I had to continue to push past my fears. After deliberately deciding to move forward in the direction I intuitively felt was right, I became a new person. I was on my way to free myself from the burden of helping someone else build his or her dream. I started using my time and mental energy more wisely to focus on building my dreams. I realized it was time to live my real purpose. There was something else better out there calling me, and I was finally able to say I found it.

There is more to life than what you are used to. The only way to find out what life has for you is to take a risk to bet on yourself to find it.

It was time to quit my job to pursue my dreams and find out what I was made of. I understood this decision would come with some major changes. I wanted to be as prepared as I could, so I created a plan and started to follow what I call the "Dreamer's Journey." It's a process that in part consists of you being completely honest about your fears, setting goals, and holding yourself accountable for your progress. I needed to set goals, which included public speaking, business, and personal goals. I woke up one morning after a restless night of worrying about how long things would take to start taking off with my public-speaking career.

I even had a "keep-it-real" talk with myself. Have you ever had one of those talks with yourself? I was standing in front of the bathroom sink and looking into the mirror one morning. As I looked myself in the eyes, I said, "You are afraid of not knowing the outcome of taking this risk, and that is ok. That is part of the process. You are good enough. You are strong enough. You are smart enough, and you have good intentions to inspire others by sacrificing your comfort." With tears in my eyes, I said, "You can do this. You can handle anything you set your mind to achieve." You have to stop running from your fears. I had to face the man in the mirror and decide to embrace who I was and what mattered.

I had to prove to myself and to those who struggle with fears of leaving the status quo, that it is possible to live your dreams. I believed deep down in my heart that it is possible to live your dreams just like it was for Oprah Winfrey, Jim Carey, Les Brown, Steve Harvey, and so many others.

Forget the status quo. Go out and create your own life right now. Believe in yourself, and pursue your dreams. You already have it in you to be your best, but it starts right now. Decide to be conscious of your thoughts and your responses to them. Take action despite fear, and trust in your potential. Those are the essentials to the process of what I like to call the "Dreamer's Journey."

Reflective moment:

1. How can you change your life to fit more in alignment with your dreams?
2. What has worked so far, and what hasn't?
3. What are some of the biggest challenges you face?

Inspirational Moment with TL

The only fear you should have is the fear of not accomplishing what's possible. If all things are possible, then what is left to fear?

CHAPTER SEVEN: THE DAY I QUIT

As I started planning for the last day of work, the reality still hadn't set in that I was about to take the big leap. I had a plan to save the unused vacation money I was going to receive after leaving my job and drive for Uber and Lyft as a source of income. It was a temporary plan until I was able to come up with a better plan to get my business off the ground. I was also grateful to have the opportunity to do some work for my friend's business. We started our businesses around the same time.

I knew at this stage of the game, I would have to create multiple streams of income to maintain my independence. I looked for opportunities where I could make money doing what I loved or where I could make my own schedule. I also wanted to take a short vacation to give my mind a break so I could go into this new lifestyle with energy and focus. I thought it would be pretty cool to quit my job like a boss and go on vacation to celebrate my independence; so I planned to take a trip to Arizona to visit my dad for the week after leaving my job.

When I finally sat down to type up my resignation letter, it was as if I was having a tug-of-war with myself. On one end I was excited, and on the other, I was scared and nervous. The suspense of not knowing what would happen next was lingering in the forefront of my mind. I needed to just rip the Band-Aid off quickly and commit to my decision. I chose August 15 as my last day, which was one month away. It was either do this now or look back wondering *what if.* I was tired of wondering. I was still young. I was thirty-two years old with no kids. The time to act was now.

Taking a bold risk to pursue your dream can be rough at times. In the end, when all is said and done, you can either look back and feel proud that you took the big leap, or look back and regret never taking a risk to find out what life has for you. I decided to take the risk. I wanted to leave something behind for my future children, so they could see an example of what it means to have a dream and follow through with it until it becomes a reality. I wanted my future family to have ownership of something good that requires them to be selfless and give back to others. I wanted to go through the journey, so I could gain the experience to mentor others who dare to start their journey.

I believe if you enrich the lives of others, your life will be enriched in return. I wanted to leave my job on a positive note by helping someone else. I figured there are tons of people who would love to work for this large entertainment company and take my position. I felt I was just taking up space in someone else's opportunity and blocking someone from his or her dream job.

I remember a coworker named Mike. He wanted to be promoted to a higher-paying position in his department. He and I became friends. He was a father of three, a husband, and a dedicated hard worker. He had integrity, he was loyal, and he would get things done. Sometimes I felt like I was a slacker compared to his work ethic. During one of our breaks, he expressed his interest in working in my department. He said he tried interviewing for my position three years earlier but didn't get the job.

He had no clue that I was planning my exit to leave the company. Since I was leaving a very busy department, I knew my boss would need to replace me fast. I knew finding a replacement for my position and training would take several weeks.

Another coworker, the guy who helped me manage the help desk, was leaving for two weeks to go on vacation. I saw an opportunity to help Mike, so I came up with a plan. With him in mind, I knew we would need to hire a temp to help out with the workload, so I volunteered Mike.

Mike had the opportunity to fill in for two weeks. He was determined to do a good job. He enjoyed the job. I was committed to helping him get hired for the position. During a meeting with my boss, I explained how we needed help. Two people handling the workload was no longer enough. I asked if he would consider hiring a third person. I suggested Mike be considered for the third opening, in case I decided to chicken out and not quit my job. At least if I decided to stay, I'd have more help with Mike on the team.

During those two weeks with Mike helping out, he went above and beyond his duties. He caught on quickly. I was finally ready to deliver the news to my boss that I was leaving the company. Nervous as hell but ready to move on, I walked into my boss's office and handed in my resignation letter. I could feel my heart beating through my teeth. After I delivered the news, I made a recommendation for my replacement. My old boss said, "Sure, who do you have in mind?" I told him, Mike. To my surprise, he said, " Ok, I'll give him a shot." I was happy because I was able to end on a good note by helping someone else. Now it was time to transition into my Dreamer's Journey.

Mike was happy, and his face lit up every time we talked about the potential of him being in this new job role. It was finally becoming a reality after three years. It was a bittersweet ending. I learned a lot about myself and what was important to me during this experience. I went through a lot dealing with different jobs over the years and with my boss's personality. It was something I had to go through to have my breakthrough. I was optimistic and ready to take on my new life.

On the last day of work, I had so many mixed emotions all at once. I was happy, nervous, anxious, excited, and scared all at once. I found it very challenging to contain the collection of emotions that I had been holding on to for several months. I needed to do something about it. As I said goodbye to some of my team members, I left them with an inspirational message to encourage them to pursue their dreams. As I drove out of the parking lot looking back in my rearview mirror, I looked myself in the eyes and said, "You did it. Great job, Tommy."

Filled with overwhelming emotions, I drove over to Griffith Park by the Los Angeles Zoo. I parked my car and immediately began running through the park as fast as I could. I had no destination. All I knew was that I had to release this big ball of tension, stress, anxiety, and worry—mixed with happiness, joy, and a sense of liberation that I was feeling all at once.

It was like a scene out of the movie *Forrest Gump*. It felt like I ran three thousand miles across the country that day. I couldn't stop running. I ran so far and so fast until I was exhausted and couldn't catch my breath. I stopped to rest for a moment. I looked back and saw how far I had run. It was only about a mile, but I remember saying to myself, "Damn, I got to repeat that all over again to get back to my car?" The good news—my tension was gone. The bad news—I set myself up by running that far. You're probably thinking that's not far, but I wasn't a track star. I felt every single inch of that mile. Once I got back to my car, I released a deep sigh of relief. I remember having a sudden feeling of calmness starting to fill my entire body and mind.

It was as if the weight of the past two years had been suddenly lifted off my shoulders. There was a wide-open path to freedom with a light shining at the end of the road to guide me. I decided from that moment on, I would no longer question my decisions nor be concerned with what could go wrong. I started to trust my intuition as part of my survival. I knew that for me to become successful, I had to be confident in myself and believe in my journey. I demanded myself to think positively, pay attention to opportunities, think about increase and not decrease, and find support. I needed to use my creative mind and communication skills to create the life I desired as an entrepreneur, inspirational speaker, and author. On that hot summer day in August 2015 at Griffith Park, I promised myself I would never look back. I quit my job and said f*** it! I'm going to push past my fears and pursue my dreams.

Reflective moment:

1. What situations have you faced where you learned a life lesson?
2. What did you do about the situation?
3. What accomplishments have you had that you can give back and share with others to help them become successful?
4. What is your intuition telling you about your job? Dreams? Life? Happiness?

Signs You Are Ready To Start Pursuing Your Dreams

It is time to change things up for a short moment. Are you ready to push past your fear to pursue your dreams? Below are ten signs you may be ready to pursue your dreams. Check them out and see if you can relate to them.

Once you find the ones you can relate to, post about them on my Dreamer's Journey Facebook group page and share them with other dreamers! Do any of these sound familiar?

Sign #1: You have discontent with the way life is, compared to what you want your life to be and it stands out like a sore thumb.

Sign #2: You are focusing, more on finding answers to the question, "What is my purpose?"

Sign #3: You can acknowledge that you have a purpose and that what you currently are doing isn't fulfilling it.

Sign #4: You have a burning desire to take action to make your dream a reality but need to make more time for your dream.

Sign #5: You feel a sense of urgency to change your situation and you're on the fence about ripping the Band-Aid off to start your journey.

Sign #6: You refuse to sit back and watch others live their dreams without pursuing your dreams, or you refuse to continue helping someone else build their dreams.

Sign #7: You understand time is your greatest asset. You begin to focus more attention on priorities so you can utilize your time more effectively to start building your dreams.

Sign #8: You realize the biggest failure at this point in your life is that you haven't made an effort to pursue your dreams and you wish you would've started sooner. Good news, it's not too late you can take action now.

Sign #9: You are deliberately taking steps to control your mindset to position yourself for success.

Sign #10: You realize what you are currently experiencing is not in alignment with your dream. You also may notice how you often reflect on what life would be like if you pursue your dream.

Inspirational Moment with TL

Be the change you need, and change will come.

CHAPTER EIGHT: THE JOURNEY IS A PROCESS

I felt deep inside my heart I was making the right decisions. However, the day after I quit my job, I will never forget how I felt. I was experiencing an unsettling feeling of anxiety and worry as reality had begun to settle. I was on my own now. I had only a small plan, a vision, and a determination to create a new life. I met with family for lunch in Long Beach that day.

Everyone was happy enjoying each other's company, and here I was thinking, what the hell did I just do? I was trying my best to keep it together on the outside, but inside I was a nervous wreck. I didn't feel like eating. I wanted to socialize, but I ended up keeping to myself. All I could do was think about going away for a few days to give my mind a break, so the next day, I went to visit my dad as planned. My dad and I got a chance to spend more quality time together. I would swim in the pool while he cooked his famous barbecue ribs on the grill. We listened to music on his patio and talked about memories of me growing up. We had a good time.

After spending a week away from home, I returned to begin my Dreamer's Journey as a full-time entrepreneur and inspirational speaker. I started with a lot of momentum. I had tons of ideas and content. I volunteered to speak every chance I could find. The only flaw in my plan was that money was going out faster than it was coming in. I did everything I could to stay positive and focused on the end goal. I took full responsibility in knowing that I created this situation like I had created everything else in my life. Sometimes it can seem difficult to see positive images of how your life can be when you are dealing with how life is at the moment. I reassured myself that I would make it. I had to consciously condition my mind to stay positive.

Athletes have to go through conditioning to keep their bodies in great shape. Your mind must also be conditioned consistently to think positively, especially during challenging times. Having a few good hobbies outside of your dream is also important. One of my favorite hobbies is playing golf with my friends. I'm not a pro by any means. I just play because it's relaxing, and I enjoy hanging out with good friends. A typical golf outing consists of me meeting up with close friends and my cousin. We would discuss our future goals and business ideas while we tried our luck on the course. We support each other. We are entrepreneurs and it is not an easy transition once you've taken the leap to becoming your own boss. It takes a lot of support from friends, family, and others who understand your challenges. We were all starting our Dreamer's Journey at the same time. One friend started a medical business. Another started a graphic design business, and my cousin started his journey to become a successful comedian.

Your success is not just influenced by you but also by those you keep around you. It is very important to surround yourself with like-minded people with similar goals whom you trust. There will be times when you need each other's encouragement. True friends will always speak their truth about you with positive intent to help you stay on track or realign your focus.

While waiting for the next hole to become available, we had a conversation about the secret to how the Dreamer's Journey works. It is a process and it is all about timing. Everything happens in life at a specific time. The process of the Dreamer's Journey is a combination of visualizing, thinking, creating, learning, taking action, believing, and being patient to receive the results. Your dedication and persistence are required. It takes time for this combination to produce results. It also takes time to work on yourself to prepare for the person you have to become along the journey. If you persist, you will produce. That is the secret to the achievement of any goal. You have to trust the process and do your work.

Everything you touch, smell, feel, see, or hear is a result of a certain process that had to take place for the final product to be presented to the world. Your dream is no different. As you probably know, being on the Dreamer's Journey and pursuing a dream is not a smooth experience. It can be a very rewarding experience if you stick with it. A lot of people think they want to pursue their dreams, but as soon as they see how hard it is, and how much time and effort it takes, they don't want it anymore.

Anything good is worth working for. The hardest part is to continue to believe in yourself along the way. It's the things you don't know about yourself until you take the leap into your journey that can be most challenging to face at times. It starts with people like you and me who have ideas and goals we want to achieve. We make plans to take action, but most people never follow through. They face a roadblock in their plans or make a mistake and give up without ever learning the lesson. Those who learn from their mistakes and keep going eventually receive the benefits of their efforts.

You have to get your emotions and feelings about yourself under control to become the person you need to be to live your dreams. Your mind is your biggest asset. Everything starts in your mind, and it is up to you to take control of your biggest asset. You have to go through something in life to grow through it. I wasn't doing you or myself any justice by staying behind a desk and being a cubicle slave my whole life. There is so much life going on around you, and you cannot be a part of the experience if you hold yourself back and always play it safe. What are you thinking? Get out of your head and into your potential.

Stop chasing after the wrong things and letting fear influence your decision-making when it comes to following your passions. I allowed my fears to stop me for most of my life. Some of us point the finger at everyone else as the cause of our problems and setbacks but rarely look inward to find the real solution to the problem.

Expecting something or someone else to solve your problems is destructive thinking and will eventually drive you insane. I was waiting for a superhero to save me from the unfulfilling life no one else created but me. I had to learn to start searching from within to find answers. What is stopping you?

Now it is time to acknowledge and accept you are the solution and the problem when it comes to your thinking and your actions. You are the only one who can change them. I had to be the change I needed. You are the change you need. Stop relying on external things like people, situations, and events to validate or change you. Only you can change the things in your life that you are unhappy with. Only you can change the way you think, feel, and respond to situations or people in your life. Everything in your life starts with *you*. Be the change you need, and change will come.

The Seven Deadly Fears That Will Kill Your Dreamer's Journey

You can only change things you are aware need changing. This is why I am going to share with you the seven deadly fears that will kill your Dreamer's Journey. This will help with how you approach your fears along your journey. If I had the information I'm sharing with you in this book when I started my journey, I would have been able to position myself better. I went through the journey the hard way, and now I can help make your journey easier.

To get to the root of every fear, first, you must understand what fear is and how certain fears cause you to respond a certain way. Let's take a quick look at what fear is. Fear is an unpleasant emotion caused by the belief that something is dangerous, likely to cause pain, or a threat to our well-being. It can be a legit threat or an assumption about a specific outcome that we make up in our minds without real evidence. It is in our nature to avoid anything we believe will cause pain. When you are pursuing dreams, there are times when you have to face your fears and manage them if you ever want to move forward to the next phases of your journey. The most effective way to push past fear is to take action on it. I read a book by Susan Jeffers, PhD titled *Feel the Fear and Do it Anyway*. It is a great book that teaches dynamic techniques for turning fear into power and action. In the book she writes, "The real issue has nothing to do with the fear itself, but, rather, how we hold the fear. For some, the fear is irrelevant. For others, it creates a state of paralysis."

The most common fears we experience and allow to hold us back from pursuing a dream are the fears of failure, change, not being good enough, the unknown, judgment, rejection, and success. To some, these fears are irrelevant. To others, a simple mention of these words creates a state of paralysis. Pushing past these fears can be challenging and may seem impossible at times. If you allow fear to settle in your mind too long before taking action, it becomes a dream death sentence. The less action you take, the longer your journey will be. Without taking action at all, your dreams will never manifest themselves. This is why some people give up. All they see is nothing changing in their situation. They neglect the fact that action is required to move past these seven deadly fears. When you face your fears, you will discover a life that has been waiting for you all along.

The good news, your fears can be your greatest teacher. They teach you by helping you identify the limitations you've set in your mind. Fear teaches us that if you hide from yourself or run from the things you fear, you will never see your full potential.

Do yourself a favor: no matter how hard it may seem to start your journey to pursuing your dreams, do not ignore or run from your fears any longer. You need to take action. Your life depends on it. Your happiness and future depend on it. Your dream depends on it. It is not what you did in the past that will lead you to where you want to go now. What you did in the past was only able to get you as far as where you are right now. What you do now at this moment is what will lead you to the place you want to be in your life. You have to push past your fears.

Below I identified what I call "The Seven Deadly Fears That Will Kill Your Dreamer's Journey." Identify any similar fears you may have and declare right now that you will no longer allow these fears to stop you. From this point forward, you are a fear fighter. You must fight by taking action to push past your fears.

1. Failure

Remember when you were a child and you were told practice makes perfect? We would try so many times to practice things we wanted to be good at. If we succeeded, it felt great. We were excited and eager to share our accomplishments. What about when we failed? If we failed to do something our parents told us to do, we would be disciplined. If we failed a class in school, we would be disciplined. If we couldn't find a date for prom or didn't graduate high school we were shamed by others or shaming ourselves. We were conditioned to fear failure. The good news, failure is a good thing. It is our measuring stick. It provides evidence that there is something we need to learn to succeed. Everyone fails at something. What matters is how you handle failure and what you do about it.

2. Change

Why do we fear change? Remember when your parents used to reflect on the *good ole days*? Remember when your parents use to walk miles and miles to school in the rain, sun, and snow? Wasn't that a fun, safe time? That was when families would leave their doors unlocked and the neighbors looked out for each other. Today, it's not the same. Why do things have to change? The real question that should be asked is, "Why would I want things to stay the same?" For some, change feels like a bad thing. Changes such as relationship breakups, new jobs, or living in a new town can seem scary and hard to deal with. Change is a part of life. Nothing in life stays the same. It's the cycle of life and nature. If you are not changing you are standing still. Anything standing still and not progressing is dead. Change is necessary for growth and development. I would not be the person I am today had I continued to play it safe and chased after dead-end jobs that didn't fulfill my purpose.

3. Not being good enough

Why do we fear not being good enough? The answer is simple, but the feeling is complex. Have you ever heard the phrase "all we need is love"? At the root of your fear of not being good enough, there is a part of you, which seeks validation and acceptance. You want to be loved and to feel like you make a difference in society. When you fear not being good enough, it is a reflection of your self-confidence and esteem about yourself. You are strong. You can handle anything life throws your way. The only way you will not be good enough is if you continue to believe it.

I remember a time when I was fighting back tears as I was working on sending e-mails to schools to book a speaking gig. I wanted to book a gig so badly to prove that I was good enough. As I composed the e-mail, I was fighting with myself. I spent months preparing myself and as I finally decided to move forward, doubt started to form and I was doing my best to push through it. After sending over a hundred e-mails, I finally caught a break. A friend of mine had a contact who worked at a high school. He recommended me and a few weeks later I received a call from his friend asking me to come meet with the counselor at the high school. The meeting was a success and I booked my first high-school gig. I was excited. I felt the weight lifted from my shoulders. I accomplished another major goal and it was a huge success. I thought that I was going to the high school to inspire the students and I did, but in turn, they also inspired me. They enjoyed my talk and the teachers thanked me for bringing a valuable service to the school to help the community. This was confirmation that I was valuable. You are also valuable, you just have to believe it and take action.

4. The Unknown

Do you remember when you were a child and you wanted to go outside to play with your friends and your parents would say, "Be careful out there, you never know what could happen."

Unfortunately, most of us can't see the future. We never know what each second of the day will bring. Fear of the unknown is being afraid of anything that is beyond one's comfort level without knowing the outcome—things like getting married for the first time, getting your driver's license for the first time, going to a new country, starting a new job, or quitting your job to pursue your dreams. All of these things share at least one thing in common, the unknown. You may be in a romantic relationship with someone for many years before getting married. When you say the words "I do" at the altar, then kiss each other to seal the deal, your new life begins. From this moment, just like all the other moments leading up to this moment, you had no clue as to how everything would pan out for you and your spouse. You may have had goals and visions, but you never knew with 100 percent accuracy what the future would bring.

We are faced with millions of uncertainties in life. Even at this moment, you have no idea what could happen next, and that's OK. When you live in the now and learn to flow with the world around you, you are saying to the universe, "I may not know the outcome, but I trust in the results of what I want." When you accept this, you accept change and the unknown all at once.

5. Judgment

Remember when you were in school, and you would see kids who were bullied because of the way they were dressed, the way they talk, or the way they behaved? I know this all too well. Like most adolescents, I was teased through middle school and high school about the way I talked. I would get teased because certain groups of kids would say I talked "too proper," and I became self-conscious of that when speaking in front of people. This is what fed my fear of public speaking from an early age.

One time I was confronted by a group of boys in my grade who thought it would be funny to call me names because I was cool with a lot of the girls in our grade. They were probably jealous and thought it was funny to call me derogatory names, suggesting that I was homosexual. I was in some of the same classes as these bullies, and when the teacher called on me to answer questions or participate in discussions, I would try everything I could think of to not have to stand up to speak in front of the class. I was afraid of being judged, and I didn't want to be embarrassed in front of my peers by any of the bullies. What I realized is that people are going to judge you no matter what you do. They will judge you no matter what you say or how you look. You can either let the fear of being judged by others hinder your life, or you can decide that other people's opinions of you do not determine how you live your life.

6. Rejection

Have you ever asked someone out on a date? Has someone whom you were expecting to meet ever stood you up? Have you ever interviewed for a job and were told you were "not the right fit"? That is because rejection is your life's protection. If you were to hear someone say to you, "Rejection is your life's protection," during a time when you want something and the answer is no, you'd probably want to close this book and throw it at them. It is hard to see how rejection protects you in the moment of being rejected. It is most evident to see in the times you are presented with another opportunity or situation that is far better than what you were rejected from.

I believe rejection is a tool that the universe uses to keep us on track. However, it all depends on how you view rejection. It's like the glass is either half full or half empty point of view. Rejection can shut down circumstances that could potentially ruin your life or take you off course. On the other hand, rejection could be the thing that keeps you at a standstill preventing you from moving forward, but only because you allow it. You have complete control over how you view and respond to rejection.

7. Success

Why do we fear success? It is the result of everything we want to see accomplished. Yet, so many of us fear it. Some fear success because they are concerned about what it will do to their relationships. Some fear success because they believe they will become successful and then lose it all. At the root of this fear, there is the lack of belief in your potential. OK, so you don't want to alienate yourself from family and close friends. No one says you have to. You can be successful and still maintain your relationships. You can have success and maintain it for the rest of your life, but you have to believe in it and consistently work for it. You have to continue the actions you took to get you to success and exceed them. If you stay productive and avoid becoming complacent once you've reached your success, the sky will continue to be the limit for you.

Success is a long road trip filled with several bathroom breaks, bumps, twists, and turns. It is never a straight or short path. I must warn you. Once you prove to yourself that you can make your dreams a reality, there may be an unsettling feeling of not knowing what's next. You may even find yourself asking, "How do I keep this thing going?" If you are like how I was, you might start thinking of all the worse possible things that could go wrong.

It's important to know, the thing that feels unfamiliar to you is the success you just achieved. Embrace your achievement and feel the positive feelings associated with your victory. Remember, if you do it once you can repeat it. It may be a long road, but if you made it this far, then there is nothing else you can't do.

Ten Ways to Help You Push Past Your Fears

As I mentioned earlier, before I built enough courage to quit my job to pursue my dreams, I had to approach my fears differently. Fear is a dream killer. I know that now because I had to live in fear of pursuing my dreams for several years before I realized it was killing my dreams and me slowly.

It is time for you to let go of the fears preventing you from pursuing your dreams, and to trust in yourself, and the vision you hold for your life. The only way to do this is to address your fears. Here are ten ways to help you push past the seven deadly fears that kill every dream.

1. Acknowledge it.
You cannot overcome something until you are aware it is an issue. Which of these seven deadly fears has you been challenged with? Acknowledging your fears means you are being honest with yourself. You must identify the problem so you can move past it. Take a moment to identify your fears. How has this fear prevented you from moving forward with your dreams?

2. Make a list of negative outcomes if you do not conquer your fears. What is the worst-case scenario if you do not conquer your fears?

3. Make a list of the positive outcomes if you do conquer your fears. What will life feel like for you when you conquer your fears?

4. Take control over any negative thoughts or limiting beliefs.
Negative thinking and limiting beliefs can kill your dreams as well as your fear. Personal development books and surrounding yourself with positive successful people will help you.

5. Take action despite fear.
Remember the time to take action and live your purpose is now. Don't be afraid to take the next step. As long as it doesn't kill you, it will make you stronger. You will not overcome your fears until you take action.

6. Focus on the small and big victories surrounding your choice to push past your fears.
Start training your mind to seek victories in everything you do. Always remember to acknowledge any victories surrounding your efforts to push past your fears.

7. Surround yourself with people who support your efforts to push past your fear.
This is important to repeat. Find a social network or a group of people you can feel comfortable with sharing your challenges. Toastmasters International is a great organization to be a part of if you are looking to work on your public-speaking fears. Find events or networking organizations that relate to what you are pursuing to meet people and build mutually supportive relationships.

8. Surround yourself with people who will hold you accountable if you start to fall off track.
This is where close relatives and friends can be very helpful when dealing with your challenges. Only surround yourself with quality people who will build you up and not tear you down.

9. Seek mentors.
Search online, and ask your network of friends or relatives to seek out a mentor. This would be someone who has already accomplished

what you are working toward, who can help guide you and share his or her experiences with you.

10. Celebrate your accomplishments by pushing past another fear.

That's right! Once you feel like you've overcome one fear, guess what you have to do next? Keep the ball rolling. Tackle your next fear or challenge with the same approach. You'll be amazed at how confident you become in the process. Work toward being fearless.

CHALLENGE #4

Think of answers to the following questions. Review your answers every day and then track your progress. Share your answers and progress with me on my "Dreamer's Journey" Facebook group page. On a sheet of paper, write down your answers. Be specific because this is your dream at stake.

1. Identify all aspects of pursuing your dream you are afraid of.
2. Identify your fears and list all the reasons why you are afraid of pursuing your dreams.
3. Challenge your list of reasons why you are afraid by making a list of negative and positive outcomes if you were to push past your fears.
4. Challenge yourself by making a list of the negative and positive outcomes if you do not push past your fears.

Inspirational Moment with TL

If there are no limits, who could you become?

CHAPTER NINE: THE DREAMER'S JOURNEY

The Dreamer's Journey is a life-changing experience. When you are pursuing your dreams and transforming your life, it requires a lifetime commitment to yourself and your dreams. It all starts with you. To move forward successfully along the journey, there are some things you will need to know about yourself to help align you with your goals. If you allow yourself to be open to the infinite possibilities of what your life could be and the infinite potential that is within you, your journey will teach you more than you could ever imagine.

This journey will help you reveal the way you think and operate when it comes to how you perceive your fears and self-limitations. It will teach you how to be in the present moment to discover who you are and what is important to you along your journey. The journey will also help you look at your thoughts to analyze them in a way to help you reframe your inner voice and take action. If you choose to continue along the journey until you reach your destination, you will discover the power of finishing one thing at a time to align you with your dream.

VISIONS OF A DREAMER

Once you begin your journey, you are a dreamer. As a dreamer, you have a vision that no one else can see like you do. It is your life's mission to make your dream a reality. It is not easy being a dreamer. As a dreamer, you must learn to fight the battle of seeing things the way you want them to be while dealing with the reality of the way things are in the present moment. You must be careful not to look at where you are currently in your life and conclude that your dream is not possible. I will stress this again because it is important to understand. The battle all successful visionaries had to face and conquer is the reoccurring cycle of pressure from seeing your world as how it could be, while still having to deal with your current reality and the life you have created up to the present moment. You want what you see and what's in your heart, but you have to complete the journey.

The most effective way to execute your dream is to create a plan. You need a plan for every goal in life. Your plan is your map of the journey, so you know which direction to go. Understand along your journey, you will have to revise your map multiple times. You may run into dead ends and roadblocks, but that is not to stop you from reaching your destination. These are signs that you need to create a detour to put yourself back on track.

It is important to remember that you are in control of your vision and what you do about it to make your dreams become a reality. Another thing to understand about the journey, you will face things that happen outside of your control. It could be an opportunity not coming through as expected. It could be not raising enough money in time to meet a deadline. It could be not making any money at all. It could be a death in the family that becomes a roadblock. It can be anything going on outside of you that presents a challenge for you to overcome. During these moments, remember there are only two things you have control over: your thoughts and the responses. Everything outside of those two things, you can't control. When things go wrong and you feel like giving up, remember you have control over how you respond to that feeling.

One thing to keep in mind is that other people's opinions about your dreams are just opinions. Understand and begin to accept that you will not be able to please everyone. Letting go of trying to please everyone will free up your mental and emotional space to focus on your dream. Put all your effort into staying focused on the outcome of your vision and doing what it takes every day to make it a reality. If you consistently do this, you will experience moments in your life that you never thought were possible. It all starts with the vision and proceeds with a plan, and no plan can be executed without action.

Inspirational Moment with TL

It only takes one idea to introduce you to the life you want to live.
Your decision to act will determine if that life becomes a reality.

PLANNING YOUR DREAMER'S JOURNEY

Before you start planning your Dreamer's Journey, you must understand that your dream is not the destination. Your dream is the journey. Your destination is the result of you following your dream. As a dreamer and visionary, you have to establish what your journey will look like so that you are not blindly taking action without a well-thought-out plan in place. A ship without a captain cannot leave the dock. If the ship has sailed and the captain bails the ship, it will eventually crash. If you don't become the captain of your journey, your ship will crash, and you will never reach your destination. The first step to planning is asking yourself, "What is my dream?"

Every successful Dreamer's Journey begins with identifying an end result. Would you drive across the country without a destination? I know some people who would and if it weren't for the signs on the road they would be completely lost. Would you drive to work every day without receiving a paycheck? I would hope the answer to that is *no*. So your Dreamer's Journey is no different; you need to define the result for your dream. Once you define the end result, it is time to strategically put your dream into a plan of action.

CHALLENGE #5

For this challenge, you will need to write your answers on a sheet of paper, or you can use your mobile device to take notes. Write down the answers for each question below. Keep in mind you are trying to identify those things you feel passionate about. The things you would love to do, that you have been thinking about but have not done because of fear and doubt. Before you write down the first answer, let's pretend no matter how big or small your dream is, you absolutely cannot fail.

1. What do you want to accomplish with your dream?

It is time to decide what your heart truly desires and take action on those desires to make them a reality. You don't have any more time to waste hoping for a miracle or waiting for someone or something to happen to get your ideas off the ground and running. Write down this question and list all of the answers you come up with. Be honest with yourself and dig deep into what you want to achieve.

2. What actions do you have to take?

Identify at least one first step you can take to jump-start your journey. You can list multiple steps but prioritize them. Then pick one to start with once you completed your list.

3. What will let you know that you have accomplished each of your goals?

You will have multiple goals you want to accomplish along your journey. You will need to establish how you will measure the success of each goal. Do you measure it by how much effort you put into it? Do you measure it against a certain outcome or result?

4. What would your life be like if you give up on your dream or never try to pursue it?

Think about it, what would life be like if you never started the journey? What would your life be like if you start the journey but give up and did not follow it the whole way through? You have to consciously think about this so you can hold yourself responsible for staying committed to the journey. No one can force you to do anything you don't want to do. You always have a choice. This means you are not a victim. You put yourself in situations based on several factors, but ultimately you are the only one who chooses your actions.

5. What will you feel like when you achieve your goals?

Try this exercise. Close your eyes and visualize for a moment the way you might feel once your dream has been achieved. What does it look like? What does it feel like? Who is around you? What challenges did you overcome to manifest your dreams? Repeat this exercise twice a day for at least five minutes.

6. What do you choose to do right now?

Seeing as how you have made it this far into the book, you must sense there is something else out there for you. If you are curious to find out what that something is and how to obtain it, continue reading and taking action on your vision.

Inspirational Moment with TL
Every day is full of new opportunities.

CHAPTER TEN: LESSONS IN THE JOURNEY

The Dreamer's Journey is not a short-lived experience. It is not an overnight success story. It is a lifetime commitment to being determined to succeed no matter what. It is full of lessons and challenges. They are all designed to help you learn and grow into the person you need to become, to manifest and maintain your dreams. I will share with you some of my lessons along my journey. Before we move forward, take out your phone and record a video clip of yourself. I know you might be thinking, "Why do I have to record myself?" Trust me on this, what you are about to do will be a powerful reminder later on your journey. Start recording yourself now and repeat the following: "I am a Dreamer with a vision for my life. I owe it to my future self and dream to ride this journey out until my dream becomes a reality. I promise I will never give up on my goals, my dreams, or myself. I am unstoppable, and I turn dreams into reality." Revisit this video frequently along your journey for motivation and to hold yourself accountable.

You can also share it on the Dreamer's Journey Facebook group page (https://www.facebook.com/groups/dreamersjourney/) along with the other dreamers.

My first biggest life lesson when I started my journey was to not look to others for validation and self-value. For most of my life, I was so concerned about what others thought about me or if I would be accepted in social groups, jobs, and personal relationships. Once I began my journey, I promised myself I would no longer be concerned about what others think about me or how I live my life. This is my life and my journey. Worrying was taking up too much unnecessary energy that could have been used more efficiently to help me create a new life for myself. It was tough at first to stop caring but I was determined. Every time I did something new like a speech, meeting new people, or sharing ideas with a group I would do these things by exuding more confidence in what I would say and do.

If you want to be more of something, you have to exude the quality of the thing you want to be before you become it. If you want to be more confident but you're not deliberate in your actions by being more confident, then you are going to be waiting for a lifetime. You have to act as the thing you want to be before you transform into the thing you want to become.

I wanted to be an inspirational speaker. I had to practice writing and delivering speeches before that became a reality. I had to become an inspirational speaker before I started making a living as an inspirational speaker, by doing the things a speaker does. I had to do several bad and unorganized speeches before I started doing good speeches. I had to hear *no* several times from decision-makers whom I was trying to book speaking gigs with before I got a *yes*. I had to be someone who seeks to book speaking gigs before I booked a speaking gig. The only way I was able to do this was to stop worrying about what others thought about me. Your dream serves a larger purpose than someone's opinion of you. Your dreams are bigger than what other people think or say about you.

The second lesson I learned was to finish what I started. I had spent most of my life starting things but never finishing them. I went to college for the first time in 2001. I was eighteen. I was like every other kid fresh out of his parent's supervision. I went party crazy. I did more drinking and partying with friends than I did studying and applying myself. I felt college wasn't for me. I wanted to be a musician and figured I wouldn't need college for that, so I dropped out after my first year. As I mentioned earlier, I took classes for audio engineering and completed nine hundred hours of work but never completed the internship that was required for me to graduate. By 2009, I finally decided it was time to finish what I started by returning to college. I had been laid off from my job and had no educational background to fall back on, so I returned to college to get a degree. I chose to study information technology security. I graduated within three years and finished something I started.

Then in 2015, I decided to go back to pursuing audio engineering with the hopes of getting a job in a recording studio. I wanted to finish what I started when I first moved to Los Angeles at nineteen. Since I quit my job I was free to do what I wanted. I saw an opportunity to pursue the very path I had run away from thirteen years prior. So here I am starting a new journey with public speaking and revisiting an old journey I gave up on years ago. I was throwing my dreams in the air to see which one landed on its feet.

One day while on my computer, I did a Google search for audio engineering jobs. I remember that day so clearly. I was excited and optimistic. I remember thinking I had finally come full circle with the one thing I gave up on and was excited to see what life will be like going forward. Little did I know I would soon find the answer. I was looking at internship job listings and I came across an ad for a recording-studio-intern position at a recording studio less than two miles from my home. I quickly created a resume along with a sample of one of my original songs. I have over five hundred originally produced songs in my catalog so you can probably imagine how hard it was to find the best song to send. After hours of looking for the right song to send, I sent off my resume and one of my songs with my fingers crossed as I hoped for the best.

Two days later I received a response and was asked to come in for an interview with the studio owner's wife. I had been to several job interviews and felt confident about this one, so I went into it with a positive attitude and nothing to lose. After the interview, I remember feeling like I killed it. I was answering her questions smoothly. I engaged her in conversation and treated her as if she was an old friend whom I had known for years. Those speaking skills I had been developing kicked into gear that day.

Another two days went by and I got a call from the studio owner's wife. She congratulated me and told me I could start working in one week. I remember feeling so excited and hopeful. They planned to schedule me for fifteen hours a week so that was perfect because I could still make time to earn money driving Lyft and Uber to pay bills. Everything happened so quickly, from the time I decided to take action to pursue this dream again, to applying for the internship, to me getting the job and working for the studio. It was all falling into place and I was so proud that I finally decided to go forward with it. I realized I am no longer that scary nineteen-year-old who was afraid to pursue his dreams. After all, I had been through, I was able to appreciate the opportunity that was in front of me.

For the first time in my life, I allowed myself to be completely open to the possibilities of what my life could turn into. On one hand, I was pursuing public speaking and starting my business, and on the other hand, I was moving forward on a dream that I had left behind years ago while accepting that I was OK with the outcome of either venture. All I knew at the time was that I wanted something positive to happen and for my dreams to come true. It seemed like every time I started to walk in my dream (take action), everything started to align with my goals and actions. It often would happen rapidly as if it was already there waiting for me, and all I had to do was show up all these years.

During my first three weeks of interning, I was excited to be in a professional recording studio. It inspired me. I got a chance to see the big mixing boards, the professional gear, and the microphones. It was a very creative atmosphere to be a part of. I was like a kid in a candy store. I remember one morning I waited until the owner and his wife left the room. I started taking selfies with the recording equipment and instruments in the background. I was sending pictures to my family and friends to show what I had accomplished. It felt good. I was ready to give my all and even more to make this work.

Then one day, the studio owner came into one of the studios I was cleaning to prepare for the next session of the day. He told me they were revising the intern schedules for me and the other eight interns. He said he would get back to us in a couple of days. I waited a couple of days anticipating what my new schedule would be. Still excited, I was hoping that I would get more time in the studio. After five days went by I started to wonder how much longer it would take to hear from the owner. I didn't want to bother him so I waited patiently to get a phone call from him. Almost two weeks went by, then I sent text messages and voicemails to follow up. After sending e-mails, texting, and calling with no response I was completely crushed and confused. I remember trying to figure out if there was something I did or didn't do that would cause him to not respond to me. I thought maybe his telling me that he had to revise my schedule was another way of saying, "Sorry we don't need your assistance any longer."

I was nervous, so I had to give myself a pep talk to keep my attitude positive and not worry about a specific outcome. I had to find peace with the situation because I had done my part by taking action. The rest was up to the universe. I remember thinking how crazy it would be to finally align myself with what I thought was my purpose, only to discover in some kind of sick twist to the story plot that this time my dream is giving up on me as payback.

After three weeks and several attempts to contact both the owner and his wife, I concluded this must not be it. This wasn't meant to be. Surprisingly, a month went by and I unexpectedly received a text message from the studio owner's wife. She told me I could come back to work in the studio and asked what was my availability for the week. Unsure of how I felt about the lack of professionalism, I ignored her for two days to think about it. I felt as though it was very unprofessional for them to leave me hanging for so long without responding to my inquiries. It said a lot about their judgment and character as business owners. When I replied two days later, I told her my schedule and availability but to no avail, she did not respond.

Two months went by, and I received another unexpected text message. This time it was from the studio owner asking me if I was available to intern for them. In my mind, I was over this internship experience due to the lack of response and poor communication on their part. I moved on to focus on public speaking. Even though I was unhappy with the way they handled things, I couldn't help to ask myself—is this fate, or is it a test? Along your journey, you will be faced with a series of tests that will either pull you closer to your dream or push you in a different direction.

When I received the owner's message, I was sitting at my computer, preparing a speech for a speech contest. I was in the third round of the competition. I had previously won first place for my speech "The Enemy Within," and I was working on my next speech, titled "Picking Up Your Dream." Since I wasn't interning, I had more time to focus on my speaking career.

After delivering my speeches, people were coming up to me to tell me how I inspired them to start thinking about their dreams and goals. I even had a nice lady by the name of Carla break down and cry after one of my speeches. She told me I helped her figure out what had been blocking her for many years from starting her business. I could see a gift that I was developing and sharing with others. I was making a positive impact on someone else's life. When I got the random text after two months from the studio owner, I felt like I was at a crossroads between two different journeys. Should I intern or should I continue building Dream2Inspire?

I had reached a definitive moment in my life. I remember sitting at my computer and listening to one of my songs called "Visions of a Dreamer," available on iTunes, Google Play, Spotify, CDBaby, and Amazon Mp3 (clear my throat and smile). You can find a link to my music at the end of the book. I was listening to my song "Visions of a Dreamer" and looking at the text message from the studio owner asking me when I was available. I was trying to decide if I should respond. At that moment, it was as if all of my dreams met with me in the middle of the road, and they were staring back at me asking, "What are you going to choose?" They were like high-school bullies ready to beat me down the moment I made a move or said a word. I needed to make a decision, and my decision needed to be based on what I felt was right within my heart to pursue.

As I reflected on my past journey, I had been down the audio engineering road before. For different reasons, I stopped pursuing it. Here I was years later, thinking that I would resume where I left off. I thought my audio engineering journey would turn out to have a happily ever after ending, but I was dealing with a new dream and passion at the same time. I was an inspirational speaker now with a business to help inspire and transform lives. I felt it was a more fulfilling path. I decided that day I would close the audio engineering chapter in my life with a sense of accomplishment, due to my efforts of giving it another shot. I can honestly say I felt at peace with my decision. It was time to focus on my new journey as an entrepreneur, inspirational speaker, and author.

Sometimes in life, you have to do what is right for your dream instead of what is right for the moment.

The third lesson I learned is that I needed to retrain my mind to find the positives in every situation. I needed to work on cutting out unnecessary negative self-talk and distractions to think more positively. It is easy to look at your dreams, see all of the obstacles in front of you, and then think of negative outcomes versus positive outcomes. It is also easy to look at your current situation and feel as though there are not enough opportunities for you. If you focus on being more positive and continue doing the work required for your dream, opportunities will present themselves.

How many times have you started working on a goal and had no idea of what the outcome would be? You managed to accomplish a little bit at a time toward your goal and eventually, the goal was achieved. One of the key things I did to help me with my public-speaking goals was to continuously practice speaking and delivering speeches. I had no idea where and what my next gig would be. I just kept focusing on creating content and preparing myself, not allowing room for my mind to wander off or be sidetracked by distractions of everything going on around me. With family, career, relationship, and financial concerns it can be very hard to focus. I had to get my mind in check. I needed to attack my mind with positive content, so I started reading more self-help books. I would read articles online about business to educate myself. I needed to eliminate all distractions to focus on things that would help push me further along my journey.

I was so committed to minimizing distractions I canceled my cable account in 2014 and haven't looked back since. I was spending too much time watching reality shows and movies. It was sickening when comparing how much time I was watching television with how much time I allocated to working on my dream. I would work eight hours a day and spend about one hour in traffic commuting to work. I would need at least two hours to relax as soon as I came home at seven o'clock in the evening. If I went grocery shopping or ran errands, I would get home even later. I would watch my favorite television shows. I would cook dinner and by the time I was able to work on my business, I was too tired and needed to go to sleep to start the cycle all over again. Something had to change, so I started by closing my cable account.

It was one of the smartest things I could have done to free up more of my time to work on my dream. I also wasn't exposing myself to the negativity in the news or on social media. When you constantly hear and see negative things, it can damage your mindset if you allow it. A lot of the news today is oversaturated with destruction, fear, and hate. This has a negative impact on your subconscious mind and can hurt you over time. I think news and social media are great inventions, but the way they are being used is often irresponsible and distressing. We could lift an entire world with more positive, supportive, and uplifting media content to influence unity and peace. News networks and social media outlets are the powerhouse, which could be used to lead a global transformation promoting love, unity, and acceptance for each other. The power of media could be used for the greater good of all humanity and inspire a different type of change in the world that is so desperately needed.

I believe more money can be made from a love-and-unity approach rather than a hate-and-fear approach. As a result of the lack of positive content and influence I see in the news and on social media, I decided to create something positive to contribute to society with Dream2Inspire LLC, and my inspirational books, and talks.

It is important for you to understand your mind holds the key to your success in everything you do in your life. If you think small, you live small. If you think big, you live big. If you think you can't do something, you most likely won't. It's that simple. When you reframe the way you think, you unlock the power to control your journey. Once you remove distractions from your life, you will be able to focus on what matters, which is having a successful journey.

DREAM ENFORCERS

Along your journey, there will be people who will unexpectedly contribute something to help you get closer to your destination. They may do or say something that helps you. They may invite you to someplace where you meet someone who helps guide you along your path. They may offer you a once-in-a-lifetime opportunity when you least expect it or need it. They are placed in your life for a specific purpose. I call these people and situations "Dream Enforcers." Dream Enforcers are the unexpected phone calls you receive to offer you a new gig. They are the job opportunities of a lifetime. They are the persons you've known most of your life who say something to you in the moment you needed them. They are the people you've known for a short period who unlock a new door for your next big break. It can be that you have an aha moment with an idea you just thought about during a conversation with someone. Dream Enforcers can be anyone or anything that contributes to keeping you on the path of your journey.

I have been able to identify several Dream Enforcers who have helped keep me on my journey. The Dream Enforcer's mission is to help you continue to learn valuable lessons about yourself and the way you approach your journey. You may know one now. You may have recently had something unexpected happen that was positive and got you excited about something. You are a Dream Enforcer for someone else's journey.

Think about that for a moment. In the bigger scheme of things, you serve a purpose for not only your life but for the lives of others. You encounter a multitude of situations every day. Each moment of your existence, you are positioned in someone else's life either for something that you need from him or her or something that he or she needs from you. For whatever reason, your two paths crossed, and now your lives are being experienced at the same moment. Think of how deep that is for a moment considering the complexity of even being born in the first place. There has to be a deeper meaning for the purpose we serve in each other's lives.

To find more Dream Enforcers for your journey, you must practice being more of a Dream Enforcer for someone else by deliberately being kind and helping others. Start paying attention to those whom you interact with daily. I challenge you to go out of your way to be nice to them. I dare you to start with your family members. Be an ear they can talk to and listen to without judgment.

I dare you to say something encouraging to your spouse to help them feel good about themselves. I dare you to speak to a stranger and say something to uplift them or find a common interest to start a new friendship. I dare you to look at yourself in the mirror every morning and say to yourself with direct eye contact, "You are smart. You are beautiful. You are confident. You are good enough. You are strong enough. You deserve what your heart desires."

This is not a game. This is your life and your dream. You need as much positive uplifting energy as you can generate but it first starts with you. Then it moves outward onto others. The more you give, the more you receive in return. It's a natural law and it is very real. Be a Dream Enforcer for others, and you will continue to come across more support to help you in return.

Inspirational Moment with TL
Control your mind, and you will have control over your life.

CHAPTER ELEVEN: IN THE PRESENT MOMENT

One of the most powerful tools you can use to help narrow your focus and keep you balanced spiritually, emotionally, and mentally is meditation. Meditation is not only good for relaxation and focus, but it is good practice for learning how to be in the present moment. By being in the present moment you can observe your thoughts and how you respond to your thoughts. Once you are aware of how certain thoughts trigger a negative response, you can make a conscious choice to respond differently.

Meditation also helps you become more aware of the fact that your breathing and your thinking are equally involuntary as they are voluntary. Meaning, you don't have to think about breathing to breathe. Just as you don't have to think about thinking to think. Things are happening to you involuntarily just as there are things you cause to happen simultaneously. This makes you and your mind extremely powerful. You gain so much more control over your journey when you accept this simple truth; there are things out of your control, and you must begin to learn how to let them go in this current moment. No more unnecessary emotional energy, no more guilt, no more worrying, or stress. Just let it go.

Another discovery to practicing being in the present moment is the delusion of time. The delusion of time is thinking you have time to waste. To think that you have time to put something off you desire is a delusion. How much time do you have? You could wake up tomorrow and your life could be over. You could finish reading this book, and something could happen to throw you a curve ball. You may say to yourself, "I'm not ready yet. I'll be ready when I can save more money, or I want to wait until next year to start my journey because this year has been rough." So what? If you are going to spend every day doing something you hate or doing something else other than what you truly desire, you are wasting precious seconds of your life you will never be able to get back. Meditation helps you center yourself and find peace in your life.

The truth of the matter is, the present moment is all you have, all you ever had, and all you will ever have. Everything you think, say, or do has always been in a "present moment." So when you consciously operate from the present moment, meaning you are fully aware of the power of choice, you may understand the urgency of following your dreams now. What you choose to think, say, and do in every moment of your life matters.

You have to commit to yourself right now that you will not waste another second, minute, hour, or day directing all of your mental, physical, and emotional energy on those things that are not in alignment with what you want your life to be. If you are working a meaningless job that doesn't fulfill a bigger purpose for your life and you hate it, then quit. If you are sick of your relationship with someone, move on. If you hate your life, then you've got a much bigger problem than what I am qualified to help you with. If you hate what you have created so far for your life or are unhappy with your current circumstances, you have the control to change them. It may not be an easy change at first. It may not be the most convenient option for change at the moment. The question you must ask yourself is, "Does it make sense for my journey and will it make me happy when it's all said and done?" If the answer is yes, go for it!

So you might be thinking, "Ok, how do I meditate?" The first thing you will need to do is find a quiet place to allow yourself to relax for at least fifteen to twenty minutes a day. I suggest in the morning before you start your day or in the evenings right as you come home. You could also try meditation before you go to bed, but I have found on several occasions it is very easy to wake up from meditating the next morning wondering what happened. I don't advise late-night meditation unless you want to fall asleep, but that defeats the purpose of this exercise. If it works for you then do what works.

Now it is time to practice meditating. Let's start by sitting in a comfortable chair with your back straight and both feet flat on the ground. Relax your arms so that they are resting on the armrests or clench your fingers together and rest your hands on your thighs with your eyes closed. You can also lie down on your back with your eyes closed and arms resting at your sides.

With your body still, start listening to all the sounds going on around you. You are listening to the general buzzing and humming of the world around you as if you are listening to your favorite song. Don't identify the sounds you hear and don't attach labels to them. Just allow the sounds to be as they are and keep your body still. It is all just sounds and vibrations. You don't need to understand anything right now, just listen. What you will notice is that you won't be able to help that you automatically begin labeling sounds. It is important that you do not attempt to force any thoughts out of your mind. Doing so will only make it more difficult to relax. As you hear these sounds and thoughts, allow them to be and observe them just for what they are as sounds and thoughts. Understand they are all happening simultaneously. Things are going on inside you just as things are happening outside of you. Look at your thoughts as just noises that are happening and all you are doing is just observing.

The next thing to focus on is your breathing. Observe how you are breathing involuntarily. Don't try to control your breathing just allow it to be as is. As you become aware of your breathing, you will become aware that both the involuntary and voluntary aspects of your breathing are all just happening and you are the observer. It is with this that you can see that everything is happening to you just as you are making things happen. Take a sound, for example. If you were to stand still with your eyes closed on the beach, you would probably hear the ocean, birds, people, and airplanes flying by but you wouldn't hear the sand. Now start walking with your eyes closed a couple of feet and notice what you hear. You begin to hear the sand because you are moving sand with your feet and it is creating a sound with a certain frequency and vibration. This vibration reaches your ears and sends a signal to your brain to process the noise and identifies what you are hearing as moving sand. So you can see as you live your life, you are creating your world just as your world helps to create you.

As you breathe and do not force your breathing, you will eventually start taking deeper breaths. As you completely inhale, don't rush to push the air out, allow it to sit for a short moment, and then allow it to fall out as you exhale. It should fall out like a deflating balloon with a slow leak. Once the air is gone, allow it to sit for a short moment and then begin to inhale. Repeat this process of listening and breathing. As you continue observing your thoughts and watching your breath, you will begin to fall into a meditative state of relaxation.

Once you feel like you are done, then it is ok to stop. You don't have to force anything but allow yourself time to get into the relaxed meditative state by following along with what I described above.

What you will gain from getting into the habit of practicing this consistently is a deeper sense of self-awareness. Meditation helps you see things clearer about yourself and the happenings of the world. Eckhart Tolle wrote a book titled *The Power of Now*. This book focuses on the importance of living in the present moment. He also has another book titled *Stillness Speaks*. In the book, he suggests always saying yes to the present moment. I have read both books and can tell you they will give you a new perspective on the power of the present moment.

The most important piece to having a successful Dreamer's Journey is to understand who you are and be open to the person you need to become along your journey to reach your goals. This can be achieved more effectively by focusing on consciously being and operating in the present moment.

CHALLENGE #6

For this challenge, you will need to write your answers on a sheet of paper, or you can use your mobile device to take notes. Write down the answers for each question below. Be honest, take your time, and be specific.

1. What did you discover about meditation?

2. How do you think meditation can help you along your journey? In life in general?
3. What realizations occurred to you while meditating?
4. What predominant thoughts did you notice?
5. How do you react when you think of these dominant thoughts?
6. What could you do differently to respond to your thinking rather than react to your thinking?

Another powerful tool to help you along your journey is books. I mentioned this earlier but I swear, up until the age of thirty, I hated reading books. It took too much time, and I never could find books I liked to read. That's because my mind wasn't open to seeking to increase my intellect. I felt I knew what I needed to know and would learn something new if I had to. I wasn't open to self-help books. I didn't know of any because books weren't my focus. As it turns out, reading a book is what started my shift from how I had been approaching my life and career.

I came across a post on someone's Facebook timeline linked to an article on businessinsider.com with the headline "21 Ways Rich People Think Differently," which caught my attention. The article included samples from a book called *How Rich People Think*, by Steve Siebold. According to the book, Steve spent nearly three decades interviewing millionaires around the world to find out what separates them from everyone else.

In Steve's book, he introduces the book by saying, "This book is not about money. It is about the mentality of the rich." He compares the middle-class and world-class mindsets about building wealth and explains the differences between each group. It is an easy read and very eye-opening if you have an open mind to a different perspective on how to create wealth for yourself. The book can help you condition your mind to think and act differently about earning money.

When you focus your attention on viewing life from different perspectives, you begin to challenge some of the things you've been told or have learned about your whole life. As you become more aware through your curiosity and discovery, you will start to view the world differently. You will view yourself differently. You will never be able to go back to the other way of thinking and doing things once you discover your truth. In one of his chapters in the book, he writes, "Self-made millionaires get rich because they're willing to bet on themselves and project their dreams, goals, and ideas into an unknown future." After reading his book, I started to question my way of thinking and my approach to earning money for a living.

I would ask questions like the following:

- Are you willing to take a risk and bet on yourself?
- Do you think you can project your dreams into an unknown future?
- Is what you created for your life this far the best you can do for yourself?
- What skills and resources do you have that you can use?
- What inspires you most?

The more I concentrated on the answers to these questions and continued to read his book, which I have read over twenty times from start to finish, the more I saw a clearer picture of my journey. I realized my happiness and wealth would come from my efforts and not from me working behind someone else's dream forty hours a week. Something about his book motivated me and got me interested in reading more books. I started reading public-speaking training books. I began studying video footage of other public speakers and taking notes.

One day while searching for more videos again on YouTube, I stumbled upon a video by one of the most powerful motivational speakers I have ever heard. His name is Eric Thomas. I mentioned him earlier when I stumbled across his talk on knowing the reasons why you want to be successful. In this video, he was talking to a group of students about a story of a young man who asked this guru to help him become successful. The guru told him he will help him become successful but he had to meet him at the beach at four in the morning. The guru began to test the young man by having the young man walk into the ocean. Once he was shoulder deep into the ocean, the guru grabbed the young man by the shoulders and submerged him under water almost drowning him to see how badly he wanted to be successful. The young man's arms were fighting to push the guru away as he was frantically trying to lift his head above water. Finally, after several seconds and almost drowning the young man, the guru pulled the boy up as he was gasping for air. The young man looked at the guru as if he were crazy for almost drowning him. He said to the guru, "What is your problem? You asked me to come out here at four in the morning just so you could try to drown me? What kind of sick person does that to people? How does this have anything to do with me becoming successful?"

The guru asked the young man, "When you were underneath the water what was the only thing you wanted to do while you were drowning?" The young man replied, "Besides wanting to kick your ass, I wanted to breathe and not drown." OK, so I added some extras to the story. The story continues and the guru said, "When you want to succeed as bad as you want to breathe, then you will become successful." Eric Thomas's message hit home with me. I felt what he said and from that moment I understood that if you truly want to become successful, you have to want it as bad as you want to breathe.

If you want your journey to be a success, you have to want it so much that your life would not be right without it and you believe there is no other choice but to make it happen. I had no idea when I was growing up that I would later become a professional speaker or an author. I was afraid of speaking in public. The fear of being judged was enough to keep me away from it. After watching his video along with other motivational speakers' videos, I saw what they were doing and I could see myself being able to do the same thing.

Reflective moment:

1. What are you willing to sacrifice for your dream no matter what it takes?
2. How badly do you want to complete your journey?
3. Who are the role models you look up to?

Inspirational Moment with TL

Who you are today does not determine who you can become, but you got to take the first step.

CHAPTER TWELVE: DREAMER'S JOURNEY PLAN

Having a road map to guide you along the journey to pursue your dreams is crucial to your success. Since time is always moving forward, there is no going backward to spend your time differently. So what does this mean? It means the way you spend your time now will determine the outcome of your life later. You must set measurable goals right now and begin keeping track of how you spend your time every day if you want your dreams to manifest.

Your Dreamer's Journey plan consists of the goals you set to help guide you toward making your dream a reality and the action you take toward those goals. You must be honest and hold yourself accountable. Whether you complete a goal on time or not, you must be honest and continue to push yourself to complete all of your goals until your dreams manifest. Only you know what your goals are. Start creating your plan right here, right now.

Below are the ten things to consider when creating your Dreamer's Journey plan.

1. Create goals with specific details and time frames. For example, your goal could be to call ten clients a week to offer services. I recommend setting daily, weekly, monthly, and yearly goals.
2. Ask a close friend, spouse, or family member to be your accountability partner to help you stay on track with your goals.
3. Create daily positive affirmations. You can set reminders on your phone to display your affirmations at a specific time and day so that you are constantly reminded. My favorites are "Making money is simple", "I am unstoppable", and "I am so happy and thankful for"…
4. Design a vision board.

5. Work on trusting in your ability to succeed by taking consistent action on your goals.
6. Know your reasons why you are pursuing your dream and allow those reasons to drive you past the hard times.
7. Make time for personal development and reading new books.
8. Control your inner voice and the conversations you have with yourself.
9. Remember your thoughts and actions determine the outcome of your life.
10. Think positive and be grateful for even the littlest things. Remind yourself you are in control and you can do this.

Never give up on your dream. You only fail when you give up on yourself or your dream. Now it is time to begin your Dreamer's Journey. I believe that if you have a dream, it is your mission to pursue it. If something is telling you deep down inside there is something else better out there for you, it is your purpose to find what that something is. The journey of pursuing a dream is not a smooth ride. It has its ups and downs, twists and turns. As you can see from my journey, there are external and internal obstacles you will encounter.

The most important thing is to remember to believe. Believe in your dream, believe in the process of the journey, and most importantly, believe in yourself. Know that you deserve and are worthy of the best that your life and your dream have to offer. Understand there is a reason why you are here and that your job is to discover why. What you believe about yourself and what you believe is possible determines the outcome of your life. If you control your mind, you will have control over your life, and the possibilities are endless. Everything starts with what you think and ends with what you do, in between is all about what you believe.

You have so much potential and power to create your life. You are strong. You are unique, and you are unstoppable, but only if you believe it. Be kind to yourself, your dreams, and to others. Until next time, I wish you a very successful journey. Visit the Dreamer's

Journey Facebook group page (www.facebook.com/groups/ dreamersjourney), and share your journey and thoughts about this book. Good luck and much success!

BONUS INSPIRATIONAL MOMENTS

STORY OF THE MYSTERIOUS MAN

There was a young man named Tim who was nineteen years old, about five foot seven, with long, dark-colored, wavy hair. He appeared to be very distraught.

He was running fast toward an older man who was standing on a sidewalk, waiting for a bus. Tim had a look of terror in his eyes, as if something was wrong or as if he had seen a ghost.

He stopped running to catch his breath, and the old man asked him, "What's wrong?"

With tears in his eyes and a shaky voice, Tim said, "I'm being followed, and I can't seem to get away."

The older man asked him, "Why is this person following you?"

Tim said, "I don't know, but I want them to go away."

The old man said, "What does he look like?"

Tim said, "I can't tell, but he is dressed in all black, covered from head to toe. I'm afraid he may do something to hurt me. I can't stay; I have to go." And Tim took off running three miles to his home.

Tired, dehydrated, and filled with anxiety, Tim stayed up all night because he feared if he dreamed, the mysterious man would catch him while asleep. The next day he started his day as usual. He caught no sight of the mysterious man since he had run home.

He got out of bed and went to the bathroom to brush his teeth. As he raised his head from the sink, he looked into the mirror in front of the sink, and his jaw dropped. He suddenly had the same look of terror on his face as he saw the mysterious figure dressed in all black, staring back at him in the mirror.

The young man could continue running, but instead, he stood his ground. He looked at the mysterious figure in all black and shouted, "What do you want from me?"

The mysterious figure with his face covered had no reply. He just stood there in silence.

The young man waited a moment and said, "Why are you following me?"

The mysterious figure still had no reply and stood in front of the young man in the mirror.

It was as if time was standing still. Then finally, the mysterious figure slowly reached over to the garment covering his face and began to reveal himself.

What Tim saw sent chills down his spine. He could not believe what he saw looking back at him through the mirror.

The mysterious figure leaned in and said to the young man with a deep dark tone in his voice, "When you stop running from what you fear, you reveal a part of you that you never knew existed."

To the young man's surprise, it was a spitting image of himself standing in the mirror. With a confused look and tears in his eyes, the young man continued looking into the mirror and said, "I don't understand; why are you following me?"

The mysterious figure paused for a few moments and then replied, "So you can finally see the part of you that wasn't afraid to face your fear."

Sometimes our fears are dressed in dark clothes and following us around, making us afraid of not only what we fear but also our dreams and ourselves.

Have you ever been afraid to face your fears? When you are ready to say, "Enough is enough. I am tired of not living my dreams or my potential", and when you are ready to face yourself in the mirror and say, "I am ready to push past my fear to pursue my dreams no matter the outcome," you will be ready to overcome your fears. But so many of us make the mistake of allowing fears to rob us of our dreams. Don't allow your fears to steal your dreams.

SELF-AFFIRMATION

I would like for you to read this next part very carefully and read it out loud. Are you ready? You can even write this down in the notes you've been taking throughout the book. You have been taking notes, right? Good—I hope so because there is so much you can gain from your Dreamer's Journey.

I want you to repeat the following affirmation out loud:

I live with purpose, and I create my destiny through my thoughts, choices, and actions.

I will be the best I can be. I will not fear what people say or what life has in store for me.

I will reach my full potential.

I will no longer let anyone define me as whom they say I should be because their opinion does not define my reality.

I define my own life, I define my own story, and most importantly *I define my own greatness*.

ARE YOU STRONG ENOUGH?

Remember one last thing before you finish reading. At the root of every fear, we often ask ourselves, "Am I strong enough?" The answer to this is and always has been *yes*. You are strong enough to handle your new job, your new business, your circumstances, your fears, your ideas, and your dreams. You have a light within you that shines brighter each time you push past fear and continue to stay on the path. Your fears will never go away; they will only become more manageable if you continue to attack them by taking action. When you push past your fears and attempt your dream, you will learn how to build confidence and power within yourself. The sooner you understand and accept this, the better you can use your fears to leverage yourself forward.

Use your fear toward making your dreams come true. Be the change you need, and take action on your dreams despite the fears and limitations you face. You have everything you need already to be successful. Believe and trust in yourself.

Thank you for taking the time to read this book. I truly hope that you feel ready to push past your fears so you can push forward to achieve your dreams.

FINAL REMARKS

I want to see you be great and live a successful life filled with happiness, success, and a sense of accomplishment. The journey does not end here. I created a workbook titled *"The Dreamer's Journey Workbook"*. This workbook is designed to help you take a deeper look into identifying what you desire most and how to tackle the fears preventing you from moving forward. If you believe in your dreams but need more tools to help you pursue your dreams, go to www.dream2inspirellc.com and purchase my workbook to continue uncovering the false expectations affecting your results along your journey.

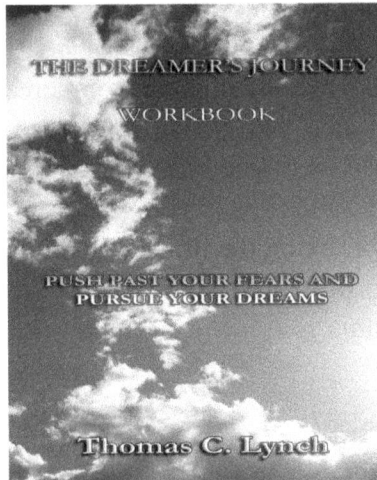

I want to hear your stories and achievements. Remember: no one has completed his or her journey alone or without support. Join the "Dreamer's Journey" Facebook group (www.facebook.com/groups/dreamersjourney) to connect with other fellow dreamers for support from the community and for sharing your journey to inspire others. Leave us your comments and share your stories with us. We love to hear your stories about your journey.

Let us know what we can do to serve you better. You can follow Dream2Inspire's Facebook page by going to www.facebook.com/dream2inspireu or follow us on Instagram and Twitter @Dream2inspireu.

Final Inspirational Moment with TL

DIAMONDS

Just like the attractive valuable diamond, you are unique.

You are worth more than what others say about you.

You are worth more than what you say about you.

So do you know your worth?

You are a valuable finely cut, rare diamond.

It is your personality, your creativity, and your

individuality that makes you special.

Know your worth.

—Thomas C. Lynch

ABOUT THE AUTHOR

Thomas C. Lynch is the founder of Dream2Inspire LLC and TL MUSIQ Productions. He is a professional public speaker, public-speaking coach, author, and music producer.

As an award-winning inspirational speaker, Thomas shares his journey and personal stories with adults and teens to inspire them to follow their hearts and pursue their dreams.

As a public-speaking coach, Thomas provides coaching and group workshops. His coaching and workshops help clients become more effective communicators and leaders in their personal and professional lives. He understands the impact that effective communication has on business, personal growth, and success. He is committed to helping you discover your most authentic self-expression as a speaker. Thomas also helps business teams enhance their communication skills to increase sales, increase customer satisfaction, and improve their bottom line.

As a music producer and stage performer, Thomas has over seventeen years of experience with music production and recording. He has recorded and released eight albums, available for sale worldwide through distribution channels like Cdbaby.com (www.cdbaby.com/artist/TL3), iTunes, Google Play, Amazon Mp3, Spotify, and other digital music distributors. His artist name is TL. To date, he continues to sell copies of his albums, "2 Night", "Ocean", "Instrumental Logic", "Instrumental Logic Vol. II", "Illusions", "Daylight", "Visions Of A Dreamer", and "Long Days Hard Nights". His music is available in the United States, Canada, Japan, the United Kingdom, and Australia.

CONNECT WITH ME

Website:
www.dream2inspirellc.com

YouTube:
Work On Your Purpose

Facebook:
www.facebook.com/dream2inspireu

Instagram:
@work.on.your.purpose
@Dream2InspireU

PUBLIC SPEAKING COACHING

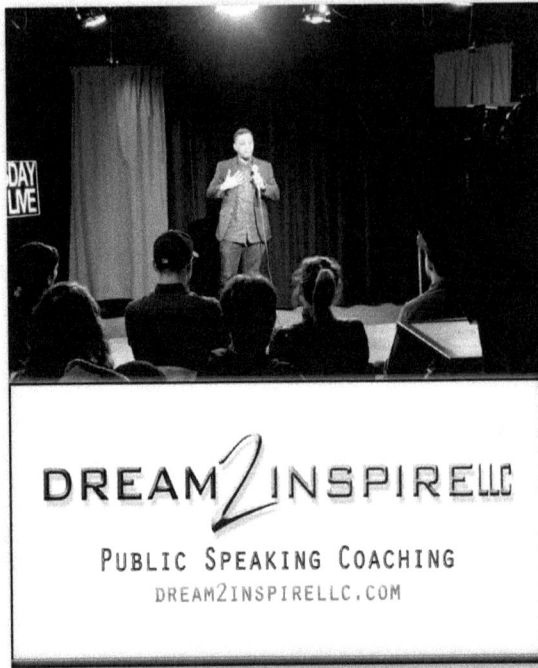

Have you ever had to speak in front of a crowd and felt your heart rate go through the roof, or felt so much anxiety you thought passing out would be a better option? I can teach you how to transform your public speaking fears into confidence, by being your most authentic self. NO gimmicks, only results. You will also learn how to use storytelling, and how to add humor to your presentations.
Visit www.dream2inspirellc.com to start your training today!

SPECIAL OFFER
DOWNLOAD **FREE** E-BOOK

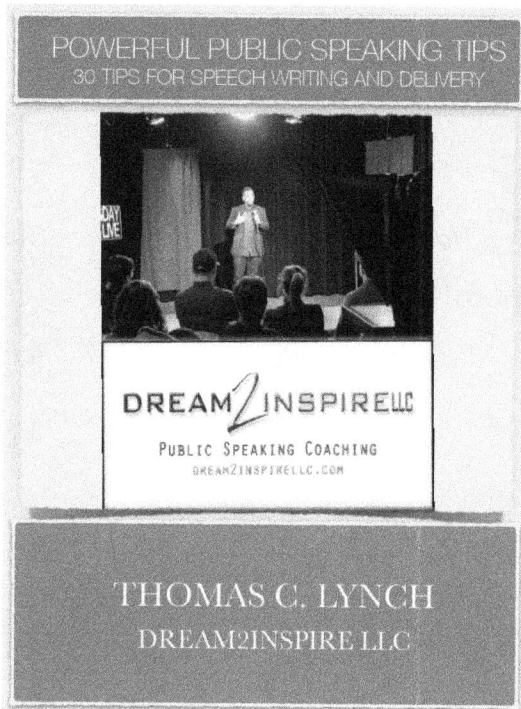

Visit www.dream2inspirellc.com/e-book to download your free copy of 30 Powerful Public Speaking Tips for Speech Writing and Delivery.

REFERENCES

Harvey, Steve. *Jump: Take The Leap Of Faith to Achieve Your Life of Abundance. (New York: Harper Collins Publisher Inc., 2016)*

Jeffers, Susan Ph.D. *Feel the Fear and Do It Anyway®*. (Ballantine Books, 2006)

Siebold, Steve. *How Rich People Think. (London House Press, 2016)*

Thomas, Eric. 2012. *Guru Story.*

Williamson, Marianne. *A Return to Love: Reflections on the Principles of* A Course in Miracles. (Harper Collins, 1996)

CREDITS

Published by: Dream2Inspire, LLC.

Cover design by: Thomas C. Lynch

Edited by: Create Space and Samica S. Taylor

Headshot photography by: Djoser Garrison-Quick

Logo by: Montae Scott and 61Elite Studios

COPYRIGHT

The Dreamer's Journey: Push Past Your Fears and Pursue Your Dreams. Copyright © 2017 by Thomas C. Lynch. All rights reserved.

ISBN: 0692847588
ISBN-13: 978-0692847589

THANK YOU FOR READING.

GOOD LUCK ON YOUR JOURNEY!

www.ingramcontent.com/pod-product-compliance
Lightning Source LLC
Chambersburg PA
CBHW062003040426
42447CB00010B/1895